Santiago Madrigal SJ

# "UNITY PREVAILS OVER CONFLICT"

## Pope Francis and Ecumenism

LIBERIA EDITRICE VATICANA

Published in Australia by

© Copyright 2019 Coventry Press

Coventry Press
33 Scoresby Road
Bayswater Vic. 3153
Australia

Original title: *El Evangelio de la Misericorida en espiritu de discernimiento. La etica social del papa Francisco*

Translation from Spanish by Guilia Tura
Translated into English by Salesians of Don Bosco of the Province of Mary Help of Christians of Australia and The Pacific

ISBN 9780648497714

© Copyright 2017 - Libreria Editrice Vaticana
00120 Città del Vaticano
Tel. 06.698.81032 - Fax 06.698.84716
commerciale.lev@spc.va

All rights reserved. Other than for the purposes and subject to the conditions prescribed under the *Copyright Act*, no part of this publication may be reproduced, stored in a retrieval system, or transmitted in any form or by any means, electronic, mechanical, photocopying, recording or otherwise, without the prior permission of the publisher.

Cataloguing-in-Publication entry is available from the National Library of Australia http:/catalogue.nla.gov.au/.

Printed in Australia

www.coventrypress.com.au

## SERIES
## *THE THEOLOGY OF POPE FRANCIS*

- JURGEN WERBICK: *God's weakness for humankind.* Pope Francis' view of God

- LUCIO CASULA: *Faces, gestures and places.* Pope Francis' Christology

- PETER HÜNERMANN: *Human beings according to Christ today.* Pope Francis' Anthropology

- ROBERTO REPOLE: *The dream of a gospel-inspired Church.* Pope Francis' Ecclesiology

- CARLOS GALLI: *Christ, Mary, the Church and the peoples.* Pope Francis' Mariology

- SANTIAGO MADRIGAL TERRAZAS: *'Unity Prevails over Conflict'.* Pope Francis' Ecumenism

- ARISTIDE FUMAGALLI: *Journeying in love.* Pope Francis' Moral Theology

- JUAN CARLOS SCANNONE: *The Gospel of Mercy in the spirit of discernment.* Pope Francis' Social Ethics

- MARINELLA PERRONI: *Kerygma and prophecy.* Pope Francis' Biblical Hermeneutics

- PIERO CODA: *'The Church is the Gospel'.* At the sources of Pope Francis' theology

- MARKO IVAN RUPNIK: *According to the Spirit.* Spiritual theology on the move with Pope Francis' Church

# ABBREVIATIONS

| | |
|---|---|
| AL | *Amoris Laetitia* |
| EG | *Evangelii Gaudium* |
| EN | *Evangelii Nuntiandi* |
| LF | *Lumen Fidei* |
| LG | *Lumen Gentium* |
| LS | *Laudato Si'* |
| MeM | *Misericordia et Misera* |
| MM | *Mater et Magistra* |
| MV | *Misericordiae Vultus* |
| RM | *Redemptoris Mater* |
| SE | *Spiritual Exercises* |
| UR | *Unitatis Redintegratio* |
| UUS | *Ut Unum Sint* |

# PREFACE TO THE SERIES

From the time of his first appearance in St Peter's Square on the evening of his election, it was more than clear that Francis' pontificate would be adopting a new style. His modest apparel, calling himself the Bishop of Rome, asking the people to pray for him – in the 'deafening silence' of a packed square – and greeting them with a simple '*buonasera*' (good evening) … these were all eloquent signs of the fact that there was a change taking place in the way the Pope related to people, and thus in the 'language' used.

The gestures and words that have followed from that occasion only confirm and strengthen this first impression. Indeed, it could be said that over the ensuing years, the image of the papacy has been decidedly transformed, involving a change that affects homilies, addresses and documents promulgated as well.

As could be predicted, this has generated divergent opinions, especially regarding his teaching. While many have in fact welcomed his magisterium with enthusiasm and deep interest, sensing the fresh wind of the gospel, some others have approached it in a more detached way and, at times, with suspicion. There has been no lack of more absolute views, even going as far as to doubt the existence of a theology in Francis' teaching.

A summary judgement of this kind could come from the very different backgrounds of Francis and his predecessor, Benedict XVI. The latter, we know, has been one of the most outstanding and important theologians of the twentieth century and undoubtedly relied on his personal theological development in his rich papal magisterium. We have not yet fully appreciated, nor will we cease to appreciate, the depth of this magisterium. What Bergoglio has behind him, on the other hand, is his long and deep-rooted experience as a religious and a pastor.

However, this does not mean that his magisterium is without a theology. The fact that he was not mostly, or only, a 'professional' theologian does not mean that his magisterium is not supported by a theology. Were this the case, we could say that, strictly speaking, the majority of his predecessors were without a theology, given that Ratzinger represents the exception rather than the rule.

In any case, the fact that we can discuss the theological significance of Francis' magisterium, as well as the fact that, very often, some of his highly evocative and very immediate expressions have been so abused as to rob them of their profundity – in the journalistic as well as the ecclesial ambit – makes the response of this series, which I have the honour of presenting, a significant one.

By drawing on the competence and rigorous study of theologians of proven worth, coming from diverse contexts, the series has sought to research the theological thinking which supports the Pope's teaching. It explores its roots, its freshness, and its continuity with earlier magisterium.

The result can be found in the eleven volumes which make up this series with its simple and direct title: 'The Theology of Pope Francis'.

They can be read independently of one another, obviously; they have been written by individual authors independently of each other. Nevertheless, the hope is that a reading of the entire series would not only be a valuable aid for grasping the theology upon which Francis' teaching is based, in the various theological fields of knowledge, but also an introduction to the key points of his thinking and teaching overall.

The intention, then, is not one of 'apologetics', and even less so is it to add further voices to the many already speaking about the Pope. The aim is to try to see, and to help others to see, what theological thinking Francis bases himself on and expresses, in such a fresh way in his teaching.

Among the many discoveries the reader could make in reading these volumes, would certainly be that of observing how so much of the beneficial freshness of the Council's teaching flows into Francis' magisterium. This is true both of the theological preparation he has had, and of what has followed from it. Given that it is perhaps still too soon for all this wealth to become common patrimony, peacefully and fully received by everyone, it should be no surprise that the Pope's teaching is sometimes not immediately understood by everyone.

By the same token, a point of no return has been reached in Francis' teaching, one that recent theology and the Council have both taught: that doctrine cannot be something extraneous to so-called pastoral theology and ministry. The truth that the Church is called to watch over is the truth of Christ's gospel, which needs to be communicated to the women and men of every time and place. This is why the task of the ecclesial magisterium must also be one of favouring this communication of the gospel. Hence, theology can never be reduced to a dry, desk-bound exercise, disconnected from the life of the people of God and its mission. This mission is that the women and men of every age encounter the perennial and inexhaustible freshness of Jesus' gospel.

Over these years there have been those who have heard some of Francis' own critical statements regarding theology or theologians, and have concluded that he holds it and them in low esteem. Perhaps a more detailed study of the Pope's teaching, such as offered by this series, could also be helpful for showing that, while we always need to be critical of a theology that loses its vital connection to the living faith of the Church, it is also essential to have a theology which takes up the task of thinking critically about this very faith, and doing so with 'creative fidelity', so that it may continue to be proclaimed.

Francis' teaching is certainly not lacking in a theology of this kind; and a theology of the kind is certainly one much desired by a magisterium such as his, which so wants God's mercy to continue to touch the minds and hearts of the women and men of our time.

Editor-in-chief
ROBERTO REPOLE

# CONTENTS

Abbreviations ................................................................ 4
Preface to the Series ..................................................... 5
    1. *Go to the land I will give you* ........................ 14
    2. *How this essay develops* ............................... 17

### Chapter 1

First words and Gestures of Francis, Bishop of Rome ............................................................. 19
    1. *Bishop of Rome* ............................................ 19
    2. *Let us begin this journey: bishop and people* . 20
    3. *'Francis, go and repair my house'* ................. 23
    4. *Custodian of creation and custodian of humankind* ..................................................... 25
    5. *Outline and preview of an ecumenical program* ........................................................ 28

### Chapter 2

The Culture of Encounter: The Ecumenical Character of the Archbishop of Buenos Aires ........................ 33
    1. *Meetings of CRECES: the **C**ommunión **R**enovada de **E**vangélicas y **C**atólicos en el **E**spiritu **S**anto or Renewed Communion of Evangelicals and Catholics in the Holy Spirit* ..................... 35

2. *Biographical episodes*.................................... 38

3. *A way of proceeding: the culture of encounter and Bergoglian priorities.* ........ 42

4. *God's 'lesson' at Aparecida: fidelity is always a change* ...................................... 48

5. *Ecumenical dialogue so that the world may believe* ............................................ 51

6. *In the wake of the Encyclical* Ut Unum Sint: *Quanta est nobis via?* ................... 54

## Chapter 3

## On the Journey to Full Communion: Speaking, Praying, Working Together ......... 57

1. *A Pope of encounter and ecumenical promoter of encounter*............................. 58

2. *The ecumenical journey of the Catholic Church and the Patriarchate of Constantinople* ....................................... 63

3. *The pilgrimage to the Holy Land: the Common Declaration of Jerusalem* ......... 67

4. *Francis and the Reformation World*............. 72

5. *The opportunity offered by the Fifth Centenary of the Lutheran Reformation: the Pope's trip to Sweden*... 77

6. *Summary. We are pilgrims and we are on pilgrimage together: peace is an art* .... 82

## Chapter 4

### Francis' Ecumenical Program: Re-reading *Evangelii Gaudium* ............................................ 85

1. *Methodological preamble: keys for interpretation* .......................................... 85
2. *The heart of the gospel and the hierarchy of truths* ................................................ 90
3. *The model of unity in reconciled diversity: the figure of the polyhedron* ...... 94
4. *The exchange of gifts: receptive ecumenism* .... 99
5. *Summary. The Holy Spirit harmonizes and reconciles diversity on the journey toward unity* ............................ 103

### Epilogue ............................................................. 111

1. *A mental representation of place* ................ 111
2. *Put a good interpretation on another's statement rather than condemning it as false* ................................................ 112
3. *The path of discernment as a means of governing* ............................................ 115
4. *'Going ahead in patience': time is greater than space.* ................................ 118

# PROLOGUE
# THE HISTORY I NEED TO CONTEMPLATE

It is just a few months since the Catholic Church entered the fifth year of pontificate of Jorge Mario Bergoglio, elected on 13 March 2013 as 'the Pope of surprises', in the words of Italian historian Andrea Riccardi.[1] In this regard we will indicate two exceptional circumstances: on the one hand we are dealing with the first Latin American, non-European pope for more than a thousand years. He has come from the ends of the earth, and looks at reality – as he likes to say – from the periphery, the outer fringes, and not from the centre. On the other hand, he is the first Jesuit pope in the Church's history, a man forged in the spirit of the mission and in the existential logic of Ignatian discernment.

What surprise has the Argentinian Pope provided us with in the broad world of ecumenism? By way of hypothesis, we could say in advance that Francis has made us feel a renewed impatience for Christian unity through his own manner and style and his own parameters, which are social harmony and peace as part of the context of constructing a culture of encounter. With a view to describing our task and the chapters in this book, this is the *leitmotiv* of the history I need to contemplate, put in the well-known terms of Saint Ignatius' *Spiritual Exercises*.

1    A Riccardi, *La sorpresa del papa Francisco: crisis y futuro de la Iglesia*, San Pablo, Madrid 2014.

## 1. *Go to the land I will give you*

The vivid image of the journey Francis made to Egypt in the recent spring, with a view to supporting Coptic Christians, certainly remains in the memory of many Christians and non-Christians, victims of a cruel attack by Islamic State which caused some thirty deaths at the Church of Sts Peter and Paul at Christmas time 2016. The object of this journey was to personally express his solidarity to Patriarch Tawadros II. On 28 April 2017, at the end of their meeting, Francis and Tawadros signed a *Common Declaration* at the Patriarchal headquarters in Cairo. They remind us in this text that 'when Christians pray together, they come to realize that what unites them is much greater than what divides them,' and they add: 'ecumenism of martyrdom unites us and encourages us along the way to peace and reconciliation.'[2]

Curiously, if we cast our minds back – and the aforementioned Declaration mentions this expressly – we see that four years earlier, on 10 May 2013, the first public meeting took place between the new pontiff and the leader of a non-Catholic Community: Tawadros II, Pope of Alexandria and head of the Orthodox Coptic Church of Egypt.[3]

We can allow these two dates to symbolically mark the *terminus a quo* and the *terminus ad quem* of the journey the

---

2   Common Declaration by His Holiness Francis and His Holiness Tawadros II, 28 April 2017.

3   Cf. AAS 105 (2013) 464-466. R Burigana, *Un cuore solo.*

Church has taken under Francis, a journey which continues, and will continue, to be open. I use the word 'journey' (*camino* in Spanish) intentionally, a term of basic spiritual significance in Jorge Mario Bergoglio's thinking: God comes out to meet us along the journey of life. He puts it very beautifully in his conversations with Jewish Rabbi Abraham Skorka:

> In my personal experience of God I cannot avoid the journey. I would say that one encounters God while journeying, being on the move, looking for him and letting oneself be sought out by him. These two journeys meet. On the one hand our journey seeking him, urged on by this instinct that flows from our heart. And afterwards when we meet, we become aware that he was first seeking us: *he took the first step.* The initial religious experience is that of the journey: 'Set out for the land I am going to give you.' It is a promise that God makes to Abraham. And in this promise, on this journey, a Covenant is established that is consolidated over the centuries. This is why I say that my experience with God comes from the journey, the search, from letting myself be sought out. It can be on different journeys, one of sorrow, happiness, light, and darkness.[4]

*Papa Francesco e l'unità della Chiesa*, Edizioni Terra Santa, Milan, 2014, 26.
    4    JM Bergoglio – A Skorka, *Sobre el cielo y la tierra*,

In the language of the Argentinian Pope, the term *'camino'* or journey serves to describe the essence of the Church, which is the people on pilgrimage to God, and the theological concept of 'ecumenism' means to walk in the presence of God. Before all else, ecumenism is a journey.

Between these two precise dates runs the history we would like to contemplate in order to feel and inwardly savour the novel dimension the current Pope has brought to progress in the ancient cause of unity. A little more than fifty years ago, the Roman Catholic Church signed its commitment to the cause of the ecumenical movement with the Council Decree *Unitatis Redintegratio* (1964). Certainly, Francis follows a form his predecessors, from Saint John XXIII to Benedict XVI, made their own by adopting the ecumenical initiatives and commitment sealed by Vatican Council II. By contrast with Ratzinger and Wojtyla, Bergoglio did not take part in Council sessions. This makes it more interesting to analyze how in practice he has taken up the ecumenical theology inspired by the Council.

As a starting point, it is worth drawing attention to his style and procedure, already shaped by his use of language 'far from the paradigm of ideas and philosophy, and decisively inserted into the living narrative of life': 'Pope Francis' language,' Spadaro explains 'is not speculative but missionary, as attentive to the interlocutor as it is to the message, spoken not to be "studied" but to be "listened to" and consequently

Debate, Barcelona 2013, 17. Available in English as *On Heaven and Earth*, Penguin Random House, New York, 2015.

addressed to whoever listens to it, and arousing a reaction.'[5] Whoever listens to him experiences the itch and impatience for unity: journeying, praying, working together.

## 2. How this essay develops

We will be reconstructing this history in four instances or chapters. In the first chapter we will recall the early steps, gestures and words of Francis' pontificate, which contain an undoubted ecumenical potential. In the second chapter, we will trace the roots of this ecumenical attitude in his life story: From whence, and how did this concern for unity originate? How did he nurture it in his years as Archbishop and Cardinal of Buenos Aires? We will see how this ecumenical engagement is part of the broader framework of his activity as leader of the Church in Argentina and as a promoter of the common good in the search for peaceful co-existence. Over the years of his intense pastoral activity which found a real point of emphasis in the Fifth General Conference of the Latin American and Caribbean Bishops at Aparecida (2007), we can also trace the embryonic notions of his ecumenical vision. Its principles were inspired by the Encyclical *Ut Unum Sint* (1995).

In a third chapter we will show Francis' personal contribution to the ecumenical cause, going back over his activity and words, meetings, texts. In the interests of brevity we will focus our analysis on the two great elements depicted in the current ecumenical panorama: the Orthodox

5 A SPADARO, *El sueño del papa Francisco. El rostro futuro de la Iglesia*, Publicaciones Claretianas, Madrid 2013, 32.

Churches and the Ecclesial Communities resulting from the Reform initiated by Luther.

Beginning with these premises, our fourth chapter deals with distilling Pope Bergoglio's ecumenical program contained in the agenda-setting document of his pontificate, the Apostolic Exhortation *Evangelii Gaudium*. Coming from a profound desire to go to the roots of the gospel, his ecumenical vision revolves around issues like: unity in diversity, the hierarchy of truths, exchange of gifts. We will conclude with an epilogue of Ignatian flavour: time is God's messenger.

The unity we seek is the fruit and gift of the Holy Spirit. Francis really believes in this Creative Spirit who makes all things new. Thus did he remind us in his homily on Pentecost Sunday, 4 June 2017. The Holy Spirit creates diversity with imagination and unpredictability, giving rise to new and different charisms. However, this same Spirit brings about unity and rebuilds harmony. He is the guarantee of the 'true unity' which is not uniformity but unity in difference. Francis returns to the words of St Cyril of Alexandria: 'Of his own accord he converts to unity those who are distinct from one another.'[6] Therefore, his ultimate message is well picked up by the exhortation to avoid two temptations: seeking diversity without unity, and unity without diversity.

Madrid, 29 June 2017, Feasts of St Peter and Paul.

---

6  FRANCIS, *Homily at the Mass for Pentecost*, 4 June 2017.

## Chapter 1
# FIRST WORDS AND GESTURES OF FRANCIS, BISHOP OF ROME

### 1. *Bishop of Rome*

On 13 March 2013, when night had already fallen in Rome, the powerful symbol of the *fumata*, the white smoke, had seen an increase in the number of faithful, and the merely curious, who had been thronging St Peter's Square throughout the day. When Jorge Mario Bergoglio, by now dressed in white, appeared on the balcony, he opened his pontificate with a simple message, 'brothers and sisters, *buonasera*,' bringing thunderous applause.[1]

With a contained emotion which allowed his humility and timidity to shine through, he underlined the fact that the conclave had fulfilled its duty of 'giving Rome a bishop,' that his brother cardinals had gone searching 'almost to the ends of the earth.' With this comment, which included a light touch of humour, he was insinuating that his electors wanted the ship that is the Church to be seen to be driven by fresh winds from the south. Thus did a way of living and understanding Christianity, inculturated within the coordinates of the Latin

---

1   Cf. AAS 105 (2013) 363. E Piqué, *Francisco. Vida y revolución*, La Esfera de los libros, Madrid 2014, 49 (available in English as *Pope Francis: Life and Revolution*, Loyola Press, Chicago 2013).

American Continent, gain prominence. This inculturation took place in the light of the new and original reception of Vatican Council II which began in Medellín (1968) and was relaunched at Aparecida (2007). In the mind of the Cardinal of Buenos Aires, geographical determination or origin is not accidental, but signifies a decisive theological qualification because – as he wrote some months later – 'Grace supposes culture and God's gift becomes flesh in the culture of those who receive it.'[2]

In an entirely natural way, the new Pope began to pray, first for his predecessor, Benedict XVI. Subsequently the new Bishop of Rome asked for the prayers of the people of God gathered in the Square.

## 2. *Let us begin this journey: bishop and people*

However, what is now interesting to emphasize are the opening words his biographers have seized upon: 'And now, we set off on this journey together, Bishop and people. This journey of the Church of Rome *which leads all the churches in its charity*. A journey of brotherhood, love and trust among us.'[3] I have italicized Francis' first words referring to the task of St Peter's successor, thoughtful words – as we will see ahead – along with the choice of his name.

They are ancient words from bishop and martyr Ignatius of Antioch's letter to the Romans, words that express in an

---

2 FRANCIS, *Evangelii Gaudium. The Joy of the Gospel*, St Paul's, Strathfield (Australian edition) 2013, no. 115 (henceforth: *EG*).

3 E PIQUÉ, *Vida y revolución* p. 34. [English edition, *Pope Francis: Life and Revolution*]

incomparable way the universal pastoral responsibility of the Bishop of Rome, and the most radical foundation of the successor of Peter's ministry.

This affirmation of the primacy in charity of the Church of Rome had been picked up in the chapter on the people of God in Vatican II's Dogmatic Constitution on the Church, *Lumen Gentium* (no. 13), to reflect the attribute of catholicity, thus recovering the notion of *communio* for ecclesiology. This same holy bishop of the early Church, when speaking of the 'immaculate unity of the Church,'[4] encouraged constant effort to achieve harmony of faith and peace. On the other hand, one cannot forget that the papal title Bishop of Rome is the one that is most acceptable in ecumenical circles for Orthodox and Lutherans.

Bishop and people: inviting the people to pray for their pastor is no trivial matter. It is to remind them of and make real the common priesthood of all the baptized, a teaching dusted off by Vatican II, which is at the heart of the Argentinian Pope's understanding of the Church. Today, after coming to know his reflections on the ecclesiological formula 'the holy and faithful people of God,' we understand better the extent of that gesture. In the interview granted Antonio Spadaro in August 2013, he explained what it means to him to think with the Church:

---

4   IGNATIUS OF ANTIOCH, Letter to the Ephesians 2,2; quoted by JM BERGOGLIO (POPE FRANCIS), in *In Él solo la esperanza. Ejercicios espirituales a los obispos españoles*, BAC, Madrid 2013, 53; 92. Available in English as *In Him Alone is Our Hope: The Church According to the Heart of Pope Francis*, Ignatius Press 2013.

> The image of the Church I like is that of the holy, faithful people of God. This is the definition I often use, and then there is that image from the Second Vatican Council's Dogmatic Constitution on the Church (no.12). Belonging to a people has a strong theological value. In the history of salvation God has saved a people. There is no full identity without belonging to a people… And the Church is the people of God on the journey through history, with joys and sorrows. Thinking with the Church, therefore, is my way of being a part of this people. And all the faithful, considered as a whole are infallible in matters of belief… through a supernatural sense of the faith of all the people walking together. This is what I understand today as the 'thinking with the Church' of which St Ignatius speaks.[5]

These words condense a good part of this Argentinian theology of the people, and the culture which accommodates the aspirations of the poor, and popular Catholicism, but it distances itself from currents of liberation theology inspired by Marxism, and sociological analysis, on the one hand, and rigid traditionalism on the other. To specify his idea of the Church, he continued by saying:[6]

---

5  Cf. A Spadaro, Interview with Pope Francis, w2.vatican.va/content/francesco/en/speeches/2013/september/documents/papa-francesco_20130921_intervista-spadaro.html

6  *Ibid.*, 259. Cf. JC Scannone, *La teología del pueblo. Raíces*

And, of course, we must be very careful not to think that this *infallibilitas* of all the faithful I am talking about in the light of Vatican II is a form of populism. No; it is the experience of 'holy mother, the hierarchical Church': as St Ignatius called it, the Church as the People of God, pastors and people together. The Church is the totality of God's people.

## 3. *'Francis, go and repair my house'*

On the other hand, Jorge Mario Bergoglio has been very aware of the extraordinary circumstances which brought about his election, that is, the historic resignation of his predecessor, theologian Pope Joseph Ratzinger, announced on 11 February 2013. He made this clear at his first meeting with journalists on 16 March. Employing a catechetical tone, he reminded them of the spiritual nature of the Church, 'the holy people of God making its way to encounter with Jesus Christ.' And he wanted to offer them a hermeneutical framework for focusing the vivid events of those days before and during the conclave: 'Christ is the Church's pastor,' and his presence comes 'through the freedom of human beings; from their midst one of them is chosen to serve as his Vicar.'[7]

---

*teológicas del Papa Francisco*, Sal Terrae, Santander 2017, 15-40. Article published in English as 'Pope Francis and the theology of the people', *Theological Studies*, March 2016, Volume: 77 issue: 1, page(s): 118-135.

7   Cf. AAS 105 (2013) 379-381. *Francisco. Palabra profética y misión*, Ediciones Copygraph, Santiago de Chile 2016, 14-15 (This is also available on the Vatican website, listed under

However, the ultimate actor is the Holy Spirit who inspired the decision of Benedict XVI and guided the choice of the cardinals.

On that occasion he explained the reasons for his choice of name. He himself joked about the suggestions some cardinals made to him: 'You should call yourself Hadrian like the great reformer' because there is need of reform. Another told him, 'Your name should be Clement, Clement XV'; 'And why that one?' 'That way you come after Clement XIV who suppressed the Jesuits.' Some thought of Francis Xavier, Francis de Sales or Francis of Assisi. By his own account, the choice of name had to do with the words of congratulation addressed to him by Brazilian Cardinal Claudio Hummes, when he obtained the majority of votes: *Do not forget the poor*. At that moment, in relation to the poor, the Cardinal of Buenos Aires thought of Francis of Assisi, the man of poverty, peace, and guardian of creation. 'Ah!' he exclaimed, 'How I would like a poor Church and a Church for the poor!'[8] No pontiff had dared use the name of the *poverello* of Assisi.

'I took his name,' he confessed in his Encyclical *Laudato Si'* (no. 10) 'as my guide and inspiration when I was elected

---

Francis' speeches: 16 March 2013, address to representatives of communication media).

8   For more details, E PIQUÉ, *Vida y revolución* p. 207-223. [English edition, *Pope Francis: Life and Revolution*]. Cf. VM FERNÁNDEZ – P RODARI, *La Iglesia del Papa Francisco. Los desafíos desde Evangelii gaudium*, San Pablo, Madrid 2014, 13-30. This is available in English as *The Francis Project: Where He Wants to Take the Church*, Paulist Press, New York, 2016.

Bishop of Rome.' It is a name which is a program of government (*nomen est omen*) as if the words the son of a rich Italian merchant heard on 1205, before the crucifix in the Church of St Damien on the outskirts of Assisi, were being re-issued: 'Francis, go and repair my house. Can you not see that it is in ruins?' The new Pope sees, in Francis, the example of care for what is weak, particular attention to God's creation and the poorest and most abandoned. He sees a mystic and pilgrim who in all simplicity experienced a marvellous harmony with God, others, nature and with himself. In that holy man we find inseparably united 'concern for nature, justice for the poor, commitment to society and interior peace' (*LS* 10).

With the passing of time we have seen that the current Pope is capable of recovering all these aspects which adorn the beautiful figure of the saint from Assisi: his concern for creation has been well reflected in his second Encyclical, *Laudato Si'*, in the same way that the Apostolic Exhortation, *Evangelii Gaudium* includes in its program of missionary reform the desire for a Church that is poor and for the poor. In the Bull *Misericordiae Vultus*, with a view to setting the Jubilee Year of Mercy in motion, he placed passionate union with Jesus Christ and his love for the least in society at the centre.

## 4. *Custodian of creation and custodian of humankind*

Once again, we turn our gaze back to the beginning of the ministry of the new 'Bishop of Rome, successor of Peter.' These are the papal titles Francis used in his first homily on 19 March, coinciding with the Solemnity of St Joseph, husband of the Virgin Mary and Patron of the Universal Church. It also coincided with his predecessor's Name day. As the central motif of his preaching, the new Pope took the figure of St Joseph, guardian of Mary and Jesus, and also – as St John Paul II reminded us – guardian and protector of the Church, the Mystical Body of Christ.[9]

From the text of the retreat that Jorge Mario Bergoglio preached to the Spanish Bishops from 15-22 January 2006, we can gather his special devotion to the figure of the Virgin Mary's spouse. On that occasion, he offered a meditation on St Joseph, taking this man who receives a mission from God to be a powerful and tangible image 'as the faithful and far-seeing *episkopo* given to the Lord in his family.'[10] However, let us return to the opening homily of his Petrine ministry.

He examines how Joseph exercised and lived his calling as guardian of Mary, Jesus and the Church with discretion, humility, in silence, faithfully and with total availability to God's plan. In this, Christ appears as the centre of the Christian vocation. However, this idea is extended to a prior dimension, a simply human one: watching over the beauty of creation and the people, especially the weakest and most fragile of them. Bergoglio emphasized an area which was given a specific reflection in his most recent Apostolic Exhortation *Amoris Laetitia*: look after one

---

9   Cf. AAS 105 (2013) 383-386 (As previously noted, available on Vatican website in English).

10   JM BERGOGLIO, *En Él solo la esperanza*, 34; 60-62. (*In Him Alone is Our Hope …* )

another (husband and wife, parents and children) in the family. In Joseph's example, concern, care, guardianship also emerge, characteristics that Francis has sought to stamp on his pontificate: a great tenderness.[11]

This is the theological framework within which the beginning of his Petrine ministry is situated, and he expressly indicated that it 'involves a certain power.' To describe this power, he appealed to the three questions Jesus put to Peter about love, followed by the threefold invitation to 'Feed my lambs, feed my sheep.' Finally, and as a culmination, he explained that 'power is service,' in these terms:

> The Pope too, when exercising power, must enter ever more fully into that service which reaches has its radiant culmination on the Cross. He must be inspired by the lowly, concrete and faithful service which marked Saint Joseph, and, like him, he must open his arms to protect all God's people and embrace with tender affection the whole of humanity, especially the poorest, the weakest, the least important, those whom Matthew lists in the final judgement on love: the hungry, the thirsty, the stranger, the naked, the sick and those in prison (cf. Mt 25:31-46). Only those who serve with love are able to protect!'[12]

---

11   Cf. W KASPER, *El papa Francisco. Revolución de la ternura y el amor*, Sal Terrae, Santander ²2015, 53-60. Available in English as *Pope Francis' Revolution of Tenderness and Love*, Paulist Press 2015.

12   FRANCIS, *Palabra profética y misión*, 13. Cf. AAS 105 (2013) 385 (also available in English on the Vatican website under

## 5. Outline and preview of an ecumenical program

Up to this point we have considered three brief addresses of Francis – from the balcony of St Peter's, the meeting with journalists, the opening Mass of his pontificate – which have enabled us to perceive in a nutshell a whole program of action, the smooth setting in motion of the revolution of mercy and tenderness with this understanding of the Bishop of Rome seen from the perspective of 'watching over' creation and humanity, taking care of the poorest especially. To these initial words and gestures we have to add his meeting with representatives of Churches, Ecclesial communities and other Religions, who took part in the opening ceremony of his pontificate. The meeting took place on 20 March. In response to the words of Bartholomew, Ecumenical Patriarch of Constantinople, he laid down the foundation of a model of apostolic fraternity for the primacy with this greeting: *my brother Andrew*. This meeting follows a tradition begun by John Paul II and continued by Benedict XVI.[13]

Francis' developed his address of reply in three parts, one for each addressee: the first was directed to Christians (delegates from the Orthodox Churches, the ancient Eastern Churches, Ecclesial Communities from the West),

---

Francis' homilies: for 19 March 2013, beginning of the Petrine Ministry).

13   R Burigana, *Un cuore solo*, 21-22. Cf. AAS 105 (2013) 420-422 (also available in English on the Vatican website under Francis' speeches: 20 March 2013, audience with representatives of Churches, etc.).

the second to Jews, and the third to the other Religions, especially Muslims.

The new Pope showed that he was moved by the presence of a broad number of communities who came to intensify their prayer for the unity of believers in Christ. Addressing himself to Christians he recalled the Year of Faith which Benedict XVI had opened on 11 October 2012, reminding them thus of the fiftieth anniversary of the beginning of Vatican Council II. He thought of the Year of Faith as a kind of pilgrimage, so that all Christians would journey together toward the centre of the Christian experience of faith, that is, the personal and transforming relationship with Christ. The desire to proclaim the nature of this encounter constitutes 'the core message of the Council' which points out to the Catholic Church its task of building visible unity in a spirit of listening, dialogue and ongoing conversion of heart. Vatican II, Bergoglio insists, constitutes a fundamental step along the ecumenical journey. Along these lines he quoted a passage from John XXIII's opening address *Gaudet Mater Ecclesia,* in which Roncalli indicated as a priority task for the Church the realization 'of the great mystery of that unity for which Jesus Christ prayed so earnestly to his heavenly Father on the eve of his great sacrifice.' All Christians are called by the Word of God to work at building up visible unity: *ut unum sint*.

A week after his election, the new Pope left a pointer to a program of ecumenical nature in the shape of this prayer:

> Let us ask the Father of mercies to enable us to
> live fully the faith graciously bestowed upon us

on the day of our Baptism and to bear witness to it freely, joyfully and courageously. This will be the best service we can offer to the cause of Christian unity, a service of hope for a world still torn by divisions, conflicts and rivalries. The more we are faithful to his will, in our thoughts, words and actions, the more we will progress, really and substantially, towards unity. For my part, I wish to assure you that, in continuity with my predecessors, it is my firm intention to pursue the path of ecumenical dialogue.[14]

In his greeting to all the Christian Communities, he also asked them for a special prayer for himself 'that I might be a pastor according to the heart of Christ.' With regard to the other religions, Bergoglio sought to give continuity to the fraternal dialogue stipulated by the Council Declaration *Nostra Aetate*. For Francis, religions should cooperate in watching over creation and caring for their common home, alleviating the material and spiritual poverty of the human being, promoting justice and reconciliation and, above all, in the struggle against economic and social systems which try to reduce the human creature to something purely material.

In setting out his program, Francis was calling on all Christians from the heart of Vatican Council II, bringing into play a series of basic elements like the joy of encounter, the need for common witness, the biblical basis of the ecumenical journey. As we will see in our next chapter,

---

14  AAS 105 (2013) 421. (Cf. Previous footnote for English reference).

all these aspects form part of the spiritual and intellectual baggage of the Archbishop of Buenos Aires, and his way of understanding and assimilating the message of his predecessors and Council teaching.

CHAPTER 2
# THE CULTURE OF ENCOUNTER: THE ECUMENICAL CHARACTER OF THE ARCHBISHOP OF BUENOS AIRES

The election of Jorge Mario Bergoglio as Pope could have been received with scepticism in some ecumenical quarters, given that it was an archbishop and cardinal coming from a Latin American country, a continent seen as predominantly Catholic. Of course, whoever knew of his activity and performance also knew that this impression contrasted greatly with the reality.[1] In this regard, Evangelina Himitian; daughter of an Evangelical Pentecostal pastor, described him in a chapter of her biographical work as 'a man for all religions,' and noted:

> As Archbishop of Buenos Aires, Bergoglio led and encouraged meetings with Jews, Muslims and Evangelicals. From the meetings of the Argentine Dialogue at which he listened to representations of different groups, to ecumenical meetings with the different creeds, they came together to discuss topics

---

1 Insisting on this is W KASPER, *Die ökumenische Vision von Papst Franziskus*, in G AUSTIN-M. SCHULZE, *Freude an Gott. Auf dem Weg zu einem lebendigen Glauben* (FS K Koch), I Herder, Freiburg 2015, 19-20.

of concern to all of society and, of course, all religious beliefs.[2]

Besides meetings with Lutherans and Orthodox, he attended and dealt directly with Pentecostal groups as we will see subsequently. On the other hand, the wide-ranging conversation with Rabbi Abraham Skorka, which became a book, takes account of his exquisite sensitivity toward other religions and especially toward the Jewish Faith. Bergoglio's introductory note is highly significant. There, he comments on the biblical tableau on the façade of the Metropolitan Cathedral of Buenos Aires, which represents the meeting between Joseph and his brothers. After decades of being apart which ended in an embrace, the tender question resounds amid their weeping: is my father still alive?

The current Pope interpreted the scene in terms of yearning for re-encounter among Argentinians, in other words, in the actual task of 'establishing a culture of encounter.'[3] However, the challenge thrown out to his compatriots is one for the long haul, and is of value to us for examining both the development of peace between nations and the attitude of dialogue between the different Churches and Ecclesial communities: Is it true that we are seeking dialogue? Do we not lack the embrace, the weeping, the question about the father, heritage, common roots?

---

2   E Himitian, *Francisco. El papa de la gente*, Aguilar Ediciones, Madrid 2013, 229.
3   JM Bergoglio – A Skorka, *Sobre el cielo y la tierra*, 13. (Cf. *On Heaven and Earth* ... )

1. *Meetings of CRECES*: the **C**ommunión **R**enovada de **E**vangélicas y **C**atólicos en el **E**spiritu **S**anto or Renewed Communion of Evangelicals and Catholics in the Holy Spirit

When tracing the profile of the new Pope, Bishop Victor Manuel Fernández, one of his collaborators, lists the following range of features: profound popular sentiment, ecclesial realism, ongoing appreciation of popular piety, sincere preference for the poor, closeness to the middle class and professional settings, personal poverty and austerity, gospel simplicity, a hierarchy of values and virtues. To this constellation of attitudes which reflect the habits of the heart of the former Cardinal of Buneos Aires, he added, last but not least, ecumenical determination and his pro-Jewish attitude.[4]

Now is not the time, nor can we undertake the task of describing this select group of vital features in a detailed manner. For the purposes of our study it is sufficient for us to consider the last of the qualities, his passion for ecumenism and inter-religious dialogue, a fact that cannot be argued with from any angle. An example is worth more than a thousand words.

Given the task of analysing what the possibilities were for Bergoglio being elected Pope, Anglo-Hispanic journalist J Burns-Marañon echoed what could be found among very critical conservative religious sectors, as exemplified by Marcelo Gonzalez. This Argentinian journalist was the

---

4   Cf. F STRAZZARI, *In Argentina per conoscere Papa Bergoglio*, Edizioni Dehoniane, Bologna 2013, 107-110.

author of an article written shortly before the Conclave for the traditional Catholic international website *Rorate Coeli*, where he maintained that Bergoglio was the worst of the likely candidates to succeed Benedict XVI. His judgement was based on the following reasons: professing teachings that are against faith and morals, using 'an ordinary' demagogic and ambiguous kind of language which turned its back on orthodoxy and Christian Tradition in the effort to seek 'an impossible and unnecessary religious dialogue: with Protestants, Muslims and Jews.[5]

The blogger was especially critical of the fact that a cardinal of the Catholic Church would have shared a stage at *Luna Park* – one of the most popular music venues in Buenos Aires – with the Evangelical Community, even being 'blessed' by a Protestant tele-evangelist. The journalist was referring to one of the fraternal gatherings organized by a group called CRECES. According to the account by Himitian, during the third ecumenical gathering in 2006, Bergoglio played a leading role in a scene which was hard to forget: when he went down to the stage 'he knelt and asked the pastors and priests to pray together for him, in a gesture of humility and unity.'[6]

---

5   Cf. J Burns-Marañón, *Franciscus. El papa de la promesa*, Stella maris, Barcelona 2016, 72; 77-78. Also available in English as *Francis: Pope of Good Promise*, Constable, 2015.

6   E Himitian, *Francisco. El papa de la gente*, 241-242. Bergoglio himself alluded to the reactions the Luna Park episode provoked: 'The following week, an article appeared entitled 'Buenos Aires, *sede vacante*. The Archbishop commits crime of apostasy" (Cf. JM Bergoglio – A Skorka, *Sobre el cielo y la tierra*, 204, or in *On Heaven and Earth* … ).

Those fraternal gatherings began in 2004. At the beginning, Bergoglio was there as just another member of the faithful, anonymously, sitting on the steps mingling with the people, benefiting from the combined devotion of Christians from different confessions but of the same faith. Himitian described the sixth CRECES event in some detail, held in October 2012, 'which Bergoglio was mentor and guarantee of.' They gathered together there as brother pastors and priests, Evangelicals and Catholics. On that occasion, Fr Rainero Cantalamessa, Preacher at the Pontifical Household, was the one leading the prayer. When his turn came, Cardinal Bergoglio transmitted his message in simple terms. The Cardinal of Buenos Aires spoke about Jesus and the time Jesus walked the streets. He said he felt fear for 'relaxed' Christians who did not come to meet Christ, and he pointed to two things we have lost: the ability to be astonished before the words of the Lord, and the ability to show tenderness like Jesus, who touched human wounds and healed them. He received thunderous applause after that brief address. The crowd recognized that this man 'had been one of the main people behind ecumenical and inter-religious dialogue in Argentina.'[7]

Without pretending to exhaust this area of research, we would like to go a little further to the roots of this tendency to dialogue. We will call firstly on some biographical episodes before considering his performance as Archbishop of Buenos Aires, his leadership of the Argentinian Bishops Conference, as also his promotion of a culture of encounter.

7  E HIMITIAN, *Francisco. El papa de la gente*, 240-241.

It is within this perspective that we need to situate his decisive role in the Fifth General Assembly of the Latin American and Caribbean Bishops Conference and its implications for the drafting of the Aparecida Document (2007) whose principles on ecumenism echo the Encyclical *Ut Unum Sint* (1995), and which continues to offer a review of the fifty years of ecumenism following Vatican II.

## 2. *Biographical episodes*

As part of this broad overview of Bergoglio's intellectual and spiritual personality, let us turn to the already mentioned book *Sobre el cielo y la tierra* which resulted from his conversations with Rabbi Skorka. It is here that we read the delightful anecdote about his first awareness of the existence of other, non-Catholic Christians at the hands of his grandmother Rosa:

> I recall on one occasion when I was with my grandmother, a great woman, and just at that moment two Salvation Army women volunteers passed ahead of us. I was five or six years old and I asked her if they were nuns. She replied: 'No, they are Protestants but they are good women.' Here was a taste of the true religion. They were good women who did good.[8]

In biographical mode, still in a recent interview before his trip to Sweden he recalled his first contact with Lutherans.[9]

---

8   BERGOGLIO – SKORKA, *Sobre el cielo y la tierra*, 78. (*On Heaven and Earth* … )
9   Cf. U. JONSSON, *Intervista a Papa Francesco. In occasione del*

When he was 17 he visited a Lutheran Church, their main Church in Buenos Aires in Esmeralda St., because on that day Axel Bachmann, a workmate of his at the laboratory, was getting married. The second memory was at the time Bergoglio was already a Jesuit and teaching at the San Miguel Faculty of Theology. Some ten kilometres away, so relatively nearby, was the Lutheran Faculty of Theology. Bergoglio invited Lutheran Professor Anders Ruuth to teach a class with him. They also shared spiritual and personal difficulties, and ended up establishing a fruitful relationship that endured over many years. The Pope continues to remember him with affection and gratitude. He also maintained good relations with Lutheran Pastor Albert Andersen from the Church of Denmark, who had invited him to preach on several occasions, and with Daniel Calvo, an Argentinian pastor from the United Evangelical Lutheran Church.

This collection of memories closes with a meeting that took place as he was leaving Buenos Aires, and was the last institutional encounter with Lutherans while Archbishop of Buenos Aires. On 'Bible Day' he says he returned to the church in Esmeralda Street where he had been the first time. There, he met theologian Mercedes Garcia Bachmann, niece of his workmate Axel Bachmann. To the question 'what can the Catholic Church learn form the Lutheran tradition?' two words come to mind for Francis: 'reform' and 'Scripture.'

We can add other information which forms part of the Pope's spirituality, In the earlier mentioned interview

*viaggio apostólico in Svezia*, in *La Civiltà Cattolica* 3994 (IV-2016) 315-317.

granted Antonio Spadaro, he mentions St Peter Faber as an ideal model of the Jesuit. He describes him with these features: 'His dialogue with all, even to the most remote and even with his opponents; his simple piety, a certain naivete perhaps, his being available, straight away, his careful interior discernment, the fact that he was a man capable of great and strong decisions but also capable of being so gentle and caring.'[10]

Regarding this restless Savoyan Jesuit, the 'reformed priest', as M. de Certeau describes him, we have to say moreover that he was the first Jesuit to come into contact with the Protestant Reformation in Germany, taking part in discussions at Worms (1540) and the Diet at Ratisbonne (1541). While reading and re-reading his *Memorial*, the young Bergoglio was able to encounter foundations for a spiritual ecumenism: Faber prayed for those who had caused the split in the Church and sought 'to love them *in veritate*.'[11]

We will close this chapter of biographical confessions with a final very important reference for our theme, which can be read in his conversations with Rabbi Skorka. In the midst of a reflection on conflict and tension in the Middle East, the Cardinal of Buenos Aires offered the following thoughts on Christian unity:

10   Cf. A SPADARO Interview with Pope Francis, w2.vatican.va/content/francesco/en/speeches/2013/september/documents/papa-francesco_20130921_intervista-spadaro.html.   See   his homily at the canonization: AAS 106 (2014) 9-11. Cf. S KIECHLE, *Grenze überschreiten. Papst Franzinkus und seine jesuitische Wurzeln*, Echter, Würzburg 2015, 55-60.

11   Cf. S MADRIGAL, *Eclesialidad, reforma y misión. El legado*

> There is a line from German Lutheran theologian Oscar Cullmann which refers to what to do to achieve unity among the various Christian denominations. He says that we are not looking for everyone, from the outset, to agree on the same principle, but propose we journey in reconciled diversity. It resolves religious conflict among the many confessions by journeying together, doing things together, praying together... It is the approach of progressing in resolution of conflict with others' capacities without overriding the different traditions nor falling into syncretism. Each, from its own identity, in reconciliation, seeking unity in truth.[12]

That is how this man expressed himself, from the end of the 1990's last century, as leader of the Church in Argentina.

Let us quickly recall the steps of this Jesuit's meteoric ecclesiastical career. On 27 June 1992, Bergoglio was consecrated Auxiliary Bishop of Buenos Aires by Cardinal Antonio Quarracino who soon made him his closest collaborator by appointing him Vicar General of the Archdiocese in December 1993. It was no surprise to anyone that he was promoted as Coadjutor Archbishop of Buenos Aires on 3 June 1997. Nine months after this appointment, Cardinal Quarracino died, on 28 February

*teológico de Ignacio de Loyola, Pedro Fabro y Francisco de Javier*, San Pablo, Madrid 2008, 143-208; here: 168.

12   Cf. BERGOGLIO – SKORKA, *Sobre el cielo y la tierra*, 201. (*On Heaven and Earth ...*)

1998, and Bergoglio succeeded him as Archbishop, Primate of Argentina, and Ordinary for the Eastern Rite faithful resident in Argentina. In February 2001, he was created cardinal by John Paul II and became titular of St Robert Bellarmine's. In 2005 he was appointed President of the Episcopal Conference, a choice confirmed for a second triennium in 2008.

## 3. *A way of proceeding: the culture of encounter and Bergoglian priorities.*

Attention can be drawn to the chapter Piqué dedicated to Bergoglio's years as archbishop in Buenos Aires, for various reasons. Firstly because the title heading it is 'An outstanding archbishop.'[13] Secondly because the Argentinian journalist highlighted two features of his personality as pastor and political animal, mixed with his charism for leadership, such that the episodes of his socio-political performance amid a serious economic crises during governments headed by Fernando de la Rúa, Carlos Menem, Eduado Duhalde and the Kirchners are combined with a handful of facts which speak of this man's vocation and ecumenical spirit, such as setting up the Argentinian Round Table Dialogue (2001) with representations from different Churches; the creation of the inter-religious Institute (2002), or the visit to the Argentinian World Jewish Association.[14] This attitude was reflected in concrete actions of mercy toward other creeds,

---

13 Cf. E PIQUÉ, *Francisco. Vida y revolución*, 133-155. (*Francis. Life and Revolution*)
14 *Ibid.*, 143-144.

including welcoming into his home a dismissed Waldensian pastor and an Anglican canon.

All this allows us to understand that the current Pope's ecumenical spirit obeys very deep convictions which come from this yearning for a culture of encounter and has shaped an attitude in him of respect, dialogue and collaboration in the political, trade union, and business life of the country, which he turned into areas of evangelization. It does not seem to me to be mere chance that the Argentinian journalist introduced, in passing, what he has called the four 'Bergoglian priorities' which take account of the fundamental principles for his way of proceeding: 'Time is greater than space'; 'Unity prevails over conflict'; 'Realities are greater than ideas'; 'The whole is greater than the part.'[15]

A detailed version of these four principles can be found in the address he gave on 16 October 2010, on the occasion of the 13th Archdiocesan Day of Social Ministry, *'Toward a Bicentenary in Justice and Solidarity 2010-2016. We as Citizens, We as People.'* There he related the four principles to the reality in his own country, where there was a need to 'carry the country on one's shoulders' to use and expression much to his liking.[16]

---

15   *Ibid.*, 142.: On the origins of these four principles, see: JC SCANONNE, *La teología del pueblo. Raíces teológicas del papa Francisco*, Sal Terrae, Santander 2017, 208-212; 253-257. ('The Theology of the People', *Theological Studies* ... )

16   An address given for the 13th Archdiocesan Day of Social Ministry, 16 October 2010: www.arzbaires.org.ar/inicio/homilias/homilias2010.htm#XIV_Jornada_Archidiocesana_de_Pastoral_Social

This address forms part of the proposal of the Argentinian Episcopal Conference, which asked that the nation's bicentenary be celebrated over a six year period (2010-2016), supported by two founding events: the 25 May 1810 Revolution in Buenos Aires, and the Congress of Tucuman which declared independence on 9 July 1816. In Strazzari's judgement, this text reflects 'the maturity of pastoral, theological, philosophical and political thinking on society understood as 'We', where citizens responsibly carry out their political vocation from within their historical and cultural belonging to the Argentinian community.'[17]

This reflection takes as its starting point the legacy of recent history which shows up wounds and unresolved questions; chronic instability and confrontations, military dictatorships, the last was over the Malvinas (Falklands), the economic crisis and depression (2001-2002). One can draw up a project for Argentina which tackles the great challenges by starting from a calm analysis. It is also a great opportunity. In his judgement, it is about working for the common good within the democratic system, looking for points of agreement and places that allow for fraternal co-existence. Behind it lies the idea of a 'culture of encounter' based on a view of the human being which seeks to overcome asocial and amoral individualism with a view to recovering the relational dimension and becoming *citizens in the bosom of the people*. So therefore it is about a process, a labour-intensive work enlightened by the four principles mentioned.

---

17  Cf. F STRAZZARI, *In Argentina per conoscere Papa Bergoglio*, 82-83.

Bergoglio explained them from this previous consideration: to succeed in constructing a common project presumes that the following three tensions between opposites can be resolved: the tension between fullness and limits to that fullness, between idea and reality, between global and local.[18]

Fullness is the desire to possess everything, while limitation is a wall set before us. Fullness is the attraction God places in the heart so we move toward what makes us free. It is the utopian dream of the common good. But limitation is the brake that restrains us. In this tension, *time* relates to fullness as an expression of the horizon, while the *moment* does so as an expression of limits. The citizen lives in the tension between the conjunction of the moment read in the light of time, the horizon. Two of the principles already enunciated come from this: first of all, time is greater than space because time begins processes while space crystallizes them; one of the sins of socio-political activity consists in privileging the spaces of power over the time required by processes.

Secondly, unity prevails over conflict. This means that if one remains in conflict, one loses the sense of unity. Conflict has to be taken on, experienced. There are various stances one can adopt to conflict: the first is to ignore it; the second is to confront it and remain a prisoner of it – but this way, one is locked in without a horizon, without any progress toward unity. The third, which helps one be a citizen, consists

---

18   As a backdrop to this way of thinking is his reading of R GUARDINI's book *El contraste: ensayo de una filosofía de lo viviente-concreto*. Cf. W KASPER, *El papa Francisco*, 39. (*Pope Francis'*

in engaging with the conflict, suffering it and resolving it, transforming it into a link in the chain, into a process.

The second tension has to do with reality and the idea. Bergoglio began with this observation: *reality* is, *idea* develops. Between the two, a dialogue needs to be established in order not to fall into nominalism or idealism.

It is dangerous to live in the world of imagination, sophism, of just the word. The idea needs to be aimed at persuading, debating, comparing ideas. That way we make progress together. The citizen must start out from reality.

The third tension looks at the relationship between globalization and localization. We need to look at the global, which always rescues us from daily pettiness and focus. At the same time, we cannot lose sight of the local, which allows us to journey without losing our sense of reality. The point of synthesis between the global and the local prevents the citizen from being caught up in the globalised universe, as illusory as is a folkloric and anarchic local focus: 'Neither the global sphere which eliminates nor the isolated particularism which cuts us off.' In the former case everyone is equal, meaning all points are equidistant from the centre of the sphere. What is the proper model for this tension, Bergoglio asked himself? 'The model is the polyhedron.' 'The polyhedron, which reflects the convergence of all its parts, each of which preserves its distinctiveness.' And he

*Revolution of Tenderness and Love*) For more information: CM GALLI, *La reforma misionera de la Iglesia según el papa Francisco*, in *La reforma y las reformas in la Iglesia*, 70-73. Also available in English as *For a Missionary Reform of the Church: The Civiltà Cattolica Seminar*, Paulist Press 2017.

added this example: 'It is the convergence of peoples who, within the universal order, maintain their own individuality; it is the sum total of persons within a society which pursues the common good.'

The 'whole' of the polyhedron, he went on to explain, is not the 'whole' of the sphere; this latter is not greater than the part but simply cancels it out. A citizen who preserves his or her personal peculiarity but remains united to a community is not cancelled out as in the sphere, but preserves the different parts of the polyhedron. To seek the union of the local in the universal, preserving the peculiar in time, means building bridges. We need to work on the small scale, in our own neighbourhood, but with a global perspective. This leads to the fourth principle: the whole is greater than the part.

Hence the conclusion: it is time to know how to plan for 'an integral development for all which privileges the struggle against inequality and poverty.' It is time to plan for 'a culture of encounter which privileges dialogue as a method, a shared search for consensus, agreement, for what unites, in place of what divides, and tackles a journey we have to take.' For this we need to prefer time to space, the whole to the part, the reality to the abstract idea, and unity to conflict.

It would be worth our while spending some time with these four priorities which trace out a project of dialogue for the people of Argentina, for peoples of the earth, for the People of God. In fact, Bergoglio incorporated them, on occasions almost literally, in his Apostolic Exhortation *Evangelii Gaudium*, his agenda-setting work (cf. *EG* 217-

237). We can anticipate that it offers us the hermeneutical criteria which allow us to translate the culture of encounter into the specific terrain of ecumenism. As we will see, he speaks of developing a 'multifaceted culture of encounter' (*EG* 220).[19] So, to understand the current Pope, we have to cast an eye for a moment on a stellar moment in the recent history of the Latin American Church.

## 4. God's 'lesson' at Aparecida: fidelity is always a change

The Fifth General Conference of Bishops of Latin America and the Caribbean took place at the Brazilian Shrine at Aparecida in May 2007. There, following the see-judge-act method, the situation in Latin America was analysed. According to data from the experts it is estimated that over recent decades the Church has lost somewhere around 20% of its faithful either to other cults or to none. From this came the idea of an increasingly missionary Church which rejects being a self-sufficient, self-referential Church in order to enter a new evangelizing stage.

As is pretty well known, Cardinal Bergoglio presided over the editorial committee which drew up the final document. In an interview with Valente he expressed his assessment of that event. In the first instance the Aparecida Conference was a moment of grace for the Latin American Church and its final document an act of its magisterium which reflects

19  On the culture of encounter, see Chapter 11 of S RUBIN – F AMBROGETTI, *El Papa Francisco. Conversaciones con Jorge Bergoglio*, Ediciones Barcelona 2013. Also available in English as *Pope Francis: Conversations with Jorge Bergoglio*, Hodder and Stoughton 2013.

harmony more than it does a synthesis.[20] A reflection on the Holy Spirit flourishes there. This is a recurring point in the pneumatological perspective of the current pope and a pillar of his ecumenical vision; the Spirit, who gives rise to plurality and diversity, can build unity, because as St Basil the Great said: *Ipse harmonia est*.[21] And Bergoglio stressed that the final Document is, in its spirit of mission, 'the *Evangelii Nuntiandi* of Latin America.'[22]

For his part, Bishop Victor Fernández comments in this regard:

> For Bergoglio, Aparecida was a powerful description of the Church's missionary calling, of the need to return to a Church which 'goes forth'. It is what John Paul II said in *Redemptoris Missio*, where he reminded us that the proclamation of the Gospel to those who are alienated 'is the prime task for the Church' (Rom 34), and that 'the missionary cause must be primary' (Rom 6). When John Paul II said these things, we did not pay attention to him. But Aparecida took it seriously that going out to seek those who have fallen away is the *paradigm for all the Church's work*.[23]

---

20   Cf. G VALENTE, *Francisco, un papa del fin del mundo*. Interviews and unpublished texts of Jorge Mario Bergoglio, Marova, Madrid 2013, 33-40.
21   *Ibid.*, 35.
22   *Ibid.*, 36.
23   VM FERNÁNDEZ – P RODARI, *La Iglesia del papa Francisco*,

The image of a 'Church which goes forth' marks the direction of the Apostolic Exhortation *Evangelii Gaudium* which is in debt to *Evangelii Nuntiandi* and *Redemptoris Missio* as we have seen. Bergoglio sums up the missionary spirit of Aparecida with a paradox: 'fidelity is always a change,' which he explains in these terms: 'to remain faithful you have to go forth,' 'because we remain, because we are faithful, we change,' 'the Lord works a change in one who is faithful to him.'[24] This would be the core of the message to Aparecida and the heart of the mission.

To get closer to the Aparecida Document is to begin to tread the terrain of Pope Francis' missionary interest, formulated at the beginning of his Apostolic Exhortation in terms of an outgoing Church. The Aparecida Document concludes by quoting a very eloquent passage from *Evangelii Nuntiandi* (no. 80):

> Let us thus recover our fervour of spirit. Let us preserve the delightful and comforting joy of evangelizing, even when it is in tears that we must sow. May it mean for us – as it did for John the Baptist, for peter and Paul,

---

48-49 (*The Francis Project* ... ). See: 5th GENERAL CONFERENCE OF THE LATIN AMERICAN AND CARIBBEAN BISHOPS, *Discípulos y misioneros de Jesucristo para que nuestros pueblos en Él tengan vida. 'Yo soy el Camino, la Verdad y la Vida' (Jn 14,6).* Concluding Document, Aparecida, 13-31 May 2007, Ed. San Pablo, Bogotá ⁵2007. The document is easily available in English as *Disciples and Missionaries of Jesus Christ so that our peoples may have life in Him. "I am the Way, the Truth and the Life" (Jn 14:6),* books.google.com.au/books?id=3c3UnQEACAAJ

24  G VALENTE, *Francisco, un papa del fin del mundo*, 36.

for the other apostles and for a multitude of splendid evangelizers all through the Church's history… May it be the great joy of our consecrated lives. And may the world of our time, which is searching sometimes with anguish, sometimes with hope, be enabled to receive the Good News not from evangelizers who are dejected, discouraged, impatient, or anxious, but from ministers of the Gospel whose lives glow with fervour, who have first received the joy of Christ, and who are willing to risk their lives so that the kingdom may be proclaimed and the Church established in the midst of the world (*DA* 552; Cf. *EN* 80).

It is not, therefore, a closed text but a text open to the mission. Ten years after the closing of Vatican II, Paul VI offered a word of advice that has lost none of its force: 'The power of evangelization will remain very much weakened if those who proclaim the gospel are divided among themselves by many kinds of divisions. Would this not be one of the great evils of evangelization?' This is why he stressed that 'the sign of unity among all Christians [is] the way and instrument of evangelization' (*EN* 77).

## 5. *Ecumenical dialogue so that the world may believe*

Using the same parameters, the Aparecida Document raised the need for ecumenical dialogue, stressing that 'lack of unity represents a scandal, a sin, and a setback in fulfilling Christ's desire: "that they may all be one, as you,

Father, are in me and I in you, that they may also be in us, that the world may believe that you sent me."' (Jn 17:21; cf. *DA* 227). This concern was placed in the chapter dedicated to the communion of missionary disciples in the Church.[25] Dialogue and ecumenical cooperation must give rise to new forms of discipleship and mission in communion. Therefore, it is 'the comprehension and practice of the ecclesiology of communion [which] leads us to ecumenical dialogue,' so that 'the relationship with baptized brothers and sisters of other Churches and ecclesial communities is a path that the disciple and missionary cannot relinquish' (*DA* 227).

When it was establishing the foundations of ecumenism, the text rejected mere sociological reasons to recall its character of 'evangelical, Trinitarian, and baptismal justification. Going back to statements from the Encyclical *Ut Unum Sint*, it reminds us that we must express, first of all 'the real albeit imperfect communion: already existing between 'those who were reborn by Baptism' (*USS* 3; cf. *DA* 228). It is necessary, then, to recover the sense of baptismal commitment. The Trinitarian and baptismal nature of the ecumenical effort is shaped through a dialogue that is a spiritual and practical attitude 'along a route of conversion and reconciliation' whose ultimate aim is the joint celebration of one and the same Eucharist.

---

25   *DA* 227-234. This chapter dedicates a section to relations with Judaism and inter-religious dialogue (cf. *DA* 235-239); previously he liked to distinguish between ecumenical dialogue and inter-religious dialogue: 'in our context, the appearance of new religious groups plus the tendency to confuse ecumenism with religious dialogue have hindered the achievement of greater results in ecumenical dialogue.'

In dialogue and ecumenical encounter, it is a case of 'living the truth in love' (Eph 4:15) so disciples and missionaries of Christ can recover the authentic meaning of apologetics as the Church Fathers practised it – as an explanation of the Faith (*DA* 229).

The Aparecida Document also invites us to recover the importance of *spiritual ecumenism* (cf. *UR* 8; *DA* 230), that is, conversion of heart and holiness of life, along with prayer for Christian unity, since it is the best way of recognizing that unity is, before anything else, a gift of the Holy Spirit. Of course, we should not overlook the fruits of the theological dialogue which has taken place in recent decades as a consequence of Vatican II. It is essential for all Christians to come to a better knowledge of and to know more about the declarations, bilateral and multilateral agreements reached by the Catholic Church with its ecumenical partners. It is timely to be informed of the directives on catechesis, liturgy, priestly and pastoral formation offered by the *Ecumenical Directory*. Certainly, human mobility offers a very propitious occasion for the ecumenical dialogue of life (cf. *DA* 231). Hence the encouragement to all (ministers, lay members, consecrated men and women) to take part in ecumenical bodies and carry out joint activities in the various fields of ecclesial, pastoral and social life (*DA* 232). Bishops Conferences are to undertake promotion of Christian unity following the exhortations of recent popes, John Paul II, and Benedict XVI, so as to patiently advance along the journey to unity.

6. *In the wake of the Encyclical* Ut Unum Sint: *Quanta est nobis via?*

When Aparecida speaks of ecumenism as a 'path that cannot be relinquished' for today's Christian, it does so in the wake of the Encyclical *Ut Unum Sint* (no. 2, 79) by St John Paul II. Undoubtedly, his body of teaching accompanied and inspired the performance of the Archbishop and Cardinal of Buenos Aires. The last part of the Encyclical on ecumenical commitment by St John Paul II opens with a question: *Quanta est nobis via?* Meaning, what is the way for us to take? This section contains various elements which inspire Francis' ecumenical spirit. In presenting the ecumenical thinking of Aparecida, the key ideas have already been indicated: personal conversion and seeking communion, whence the successor of the Bishop of Rome is called to carry out a special role. This is why I limit myself to selecting just two elements.

On the one hand, there is a notable connection established between the exercise of primacy on the part of Peter's successor, and mercy. We must not forget that Pope Wojtyla dedicated one of his encyclicals to mercy. The Bishop of Rome exercises a ministry which has its origin in God's mercy. The biblical texts speak of Peter's triple profession of love, corresponding to his triple denial. The successor of Peter knows that his ministry is one born of an act of Christ's mercy. As a consequence he knows he needs to be a sign of mercy. The Encyclical *Ut Unum Sint* indicates that the authority belonging to this ministry is at the service of God's mysterious plan 'which converts hearts and pours fourth the power of grace where the disciple experiences the bitter taste of his personal weakness and helplessness' (*UUS* 92).

Secondly, Francis' vision of the Petrine ministry revolves around the goal he himself established for the Church: *pastoral conversion*.[26] This is how he put it in his Apostolic Exhortation *Evangelii Gaudium* (24-11-2013) making his own some words from St John Paul II's ecumenical Encyclical *Ut Unum Sint*:

> Since I am called to put into practice what I ask of others, I too must think about a conversion of the papacy. It is my duty, as the Bishop of Rome, to be open to suggestions which can help make the exercise of my ministry more faithful to the meaning which Jesus Christ wished to give it and to the present needs of evangelization. Pope John Paul II asked for help in finding 'a way of exercising the primacy which, while in no way renouncing what is essential to its mission, is nonetheless open to a new situation' (*USS* 95). We have made little progress in this regard. The papacy and the central structures of the universal Church also need to hear the call to pastoral conversion (*EG* 32).

These statements presume the complete doctrinal framework which sustains the ecclesiological vision of the

26 As A. Bentué has reminded us, the expression 'pastoral conversion' used at Aparecida and by Pope Francis seems to

primacy and the episcopacy just as it was formulated by Vatican Council I (1869-1870), reworked by Vatican Council II (1962-1965) in terms of collegiality, and repositioned by the Encyclical *Ut Unum Sint* (1995) in ecumenical terms and at the heart of an ecclesiology of communion.[27] The ecumenical dimension has been transformed into an essential aspect of the ministry of the Bishop of Rome as we will see in the coming chapters, Francis is convinced that the ecumenical journey is helping to achieve a deeper understanding of the successor of Peter's service to the unity of the universal Church.

---

have been used for the first time in the final Document of Santo Domingo: 'Thus new evangelization would continue within the context of the incarnation of the Word. New Evangelization requires the Church's pastoral conversion' (no. 30) See: *Francisco. Palabra profética y misión*, 168-171.

27  On this point, see: S MADRIGAL, *El giro eclesiológico en la recepción del Vaticano II*, Sal Terrae, Santander 2017, 421-453.

CHAPTER 3
# ON THE JOURNEY TO FULL COMMUNION: SPEAKING, PRAYING, WORKING TOGETHER

In the previous chapter we presented how Cardinal Bergoglio's ecumenical character was crystallized in the laboratory that was Buenos Aires; a discerning message was distilled in the pastoral ministry of that megapolis: recover encounter through friendship and dialogue. It is the message he launched for the 12th Day of Social Ministry at the Shrine of San Cayetano: 'We need to build and establish the culture of encounter; we need to recover otherness and free ourselves from autistic approaches that close off our historical memory, close down community engagement in the present and shut off our ability to dream for the future.'[1] They were words addressed to his compatriots, but which unavoidably entail an ecumenical commitment, because to speak of building peace demands that we Christians preach by the example of ecumenical and inter-religious dialogue. For Bergoglio, ecumenism and inter-religious dialogue have been and continue to be a way of living Christianity.

Taking a step further, we would like to present his personal contribution as pope to the cause of Christian unity, his understanding and practice of ecumenism. Let us

---

1   Address by Cardinal JM Bergoglio for the 12th Day of Social Ministry, 19 September, 2009.

begin with the hopeful diagnosis of the words he uttered on 25 January 2016 at the close of the Week of Prayer for Christian Unity, during Vespers:

> While we are on the journey to full communion between us, we can already develop many forms of collaboration, move on together, and cooperate in spreading the Gospel. And by walking and working together, we become aware that we are already united in the Lord's name. Unity is achieved along the way.[2]

## 1. *A Pope of encounter and ecumenical promoter of encounter*

As we were already saying, Francis has demonstrated sensitivity from the moment he presented himself as Bishop of Rome on the balcony of St Peter's Basilica. Without saying anything substantially new, his gestures, texts, addresses express the intensity and exceptional nature of his ecumenical effort.

This was highlighted by Burigana, going back over Francis' first year of pontificate. In presenting this detailed analysis, Cardinal Kasper established these conclusions: 'Francis is a Pope of encounter and ecumenical promoter of encounter, a Pope of peace and ecumenical promoter of peace.'[3]

Francis understands his ecumenical task in continuity with the tradition marked out by his predecessors. The

---

2 Cf. AAS 108 (2016) 111.
3 Cf. R BURIGANA, *Un cuore solo*, Prólogo, 8-12.

fundamental intentions of Vatican Council II are to be put into practice and made a reality. The Council popes, John XXIIII, Paul VI and later John Paul II, opened the way to the ecumenical cause. He knows he follows in this open wake. He highlighted this on 25 January 2014, feast of the Conversion of St Paul, commenting on the contribution of St John XXIII, St John Paul and St Paul VI:

> At this time, I like to think of the work of Blessed John XXIII and Blessed John Paul II. In both of them the awareness of the urgency of the cause of unity came to maturity and, once elected as Bishops of Rome, they guided the entire flock of the Catholic Church along the path of the ecumenical movement: Pope John, by opening new ways toward this unthinkable movement, and Pope John Paul, by proposing ecumenical dialogue as an ordinary and necessary dimension of the life of each particular Church. I also locate here the part played by Pope Paul VI, another great protagonist of dialogue… The work of these Popes has seen that the dimension of ecumenical dialogue has been transformed into an essential aspect of the ministry of the Bishop of Rome, such that today the Petrine ministry would not be fully understood if this opening to dialogue with all other believers in Christ were not included. We can also say that the ecumenical journey has allowed us to deepen our understanding of the ministry of

> the successor of Peter, and we must be sure it
> will continue by behaving in this same way in
> the future.[4]

It is important to note that Francis assigns special relevance to the ecumenical journey with a view to the same configuration of the Petrine ministry in theory and practice. In the same address, he stressed that 'unity comes on the journey; the Holy Spirit achieves it along the way.' It is the journey toward reconciled diversity. He often returns to these words transformed into a kind of refrain: 'walking together, praying together, working together.'

On 30 October 2014, in an audience granted the International Conference of Old Catholic Bishops from the Utrecht Union, he developed this idea: 'The journey toward unity begins with transformation of the heart, with inner conversion. It is a spiritual journey from encounter to friendship, from friendship to fraternity, from fraternity to communion. During this process change is inevitable. We must always be ready to listen and to follow the suggestions of the Spirit who guides us to the full truth.'[5]

The former Archbishop of Buenos Aires gives great importance to spiritual ecumenism, the ecumenism of prayer, conversion of the heart, with a clear emphasis on inter-human encounter, the dialogue of charity. Of course,

---

4  Cf. AAS 106 (2014) 69-71.
5  Cf. Greeting of His Holiness Pope Francis to a Delegation of the Old Catholic Bishops Conference of the Union of Utrecht, Thursday, 30 October 2014. Available under Pope Francis' 'Speeches' for 2014 on Vatican website.

this does not mean discrediting or misunderstanding theological dialogue about doctrinal differences. Francis 'practises and also encourages us to practise a dynamic process of 'reconciled diversity' in that we journey together in the baptismal unity of Trinitarian communion – spiritual ecumenism – while at the same time being committed to ecumenical dialogue, seeking full and visible communion. Which is a gift at the service of truth.'[6]

To sum up: the dialogue of charity, or fraternal encounter, cannot be separated from the dialogue of truth, which supports and guarantees theological dialogue. This is a conviction that forms part of his ecumenical theology. This is how he expressed it, for example, in the words he spoke at the end of the Divine Liturgy in the Patriarchal Church of St George in Istanbul (Turkey) on 30 November 2014, on the feast of St Andrew.[7]

> Meeting each other, seeing each other face to face, exchanging the embrace of peace, and praying for each other, are all essential aspects

---

6  Cf. EJ ECHEVERRÍA, *El Papa Francisco. El legado del Vaticano II*, Desclée de Brouwer, Bilbao 2017, 219.

7  Cf. Divine Liturgy, address of Pope Francis, Patriarchal Church of St. George, Istanbul Sunday, 30 November 2014, on Vatican website, under 'Apostolic journeys outside Italy', 2014. He expressed himself in similar terms on 30 October 2014 before the delegation from the International Conference of Old Catholic Bishops from the Utrecht Union: 'The challenge that Catholics and Old Catholics must face consists in persevering in a substantial theological dialogue and in continuing to walk together, pray together, and work together in a deeper spirit of conversion to everything Christ wants for his Church'.

of our journey towards the restoration of full communion. All of this precedes and always accompanies that other essential aspect of this journey, namely, theological dialogue. An authentic dialogue is, in every case, an encounter between persons with a name, a face, a past, and not merely a meeting of ideas.

In the interests of very selective brevity, we will be going back over some ecumenical events where Pope Bergoglio has played a leading role over the four years of pontificate already completed. To do this we will employ the historico-theological criterion suggested by the Council's Decree on Ecumenism *Unitatis Redintegratio*. In the ecumenical dialogue set in motion by Vatican Council II, clearly two very different processes evolved: the process of reunification of East and West and the question of Catholic-Protestant ecumenism. At the basis of this asymmetry characterizing the current ecumenical situation, we encounter the history of ecclesial schisms which have seen two fundamental kinds of divisions: the break that came from Luther's Reformation represented the breakdown of structural ecclesial unity, since it affected the tradition and apostolic succession. On the contrary, the break between East and West did not alter the ecclesial structure that had developed from the second century onward.[8] There are many things in common between

---

8   Cf. J RATZINGER, «La situación ecuménica: ortodoxia, catolicismo y reforma», in: *Teoría de los principios teológicos. Materiales para una teología fundamental*, Herder, Barcelona 1985, 231-244.

the Catholic Church and the Orthodox Churches, but the chief problem is the question of the Petrine ministry.

The Decree on Ecumenism, *Unitatis Redintegratis*, was conceived according to this logic such that its Chapter Three deals with the Orthodox Churches arising from the schism of 1054, then followed by the separated Churches and Ecclesial Communities in the West resulting from the Reformation begun by Luther in 1517. We will follow this logic.

In relations between the Catholic Church and Orthodox Churches, a catalyst has been the fiftieth anniversary of the historic embrace in Jerusalem between Paul VI and Patriarch Athenagoras on 5 January 1964. With regard to the Reformed Churches, the joint commemoration of the Fifth Centenary of the Reformation is a landmark.

## 2. *The ecumenical journey of the Catholic Church and the Patriarchate of Constantinople*

Let us pick up Francis' address once more in the Patriarchal Church of St George in Istanbul. His intervention started out from this fact: 'As Archbishop of Buenos Aires, I often took part in the Divine Liturgy of the Orthodox Communities in that city.' That celebration of the feast of St Andrew happily coincided with the celebration of the fifth anniversary of the Decree on Ecumenism from Vatican II. The Pope gave a brief presentation of its content: in the Decree *Unitatis Redintegratio* the Catholic Church recognizes that the Orthodox Churches 'posses true sacraments and, above all, apostolic succession, the priesthood and the Eucharist whereby they are linked with us in closest intimacy' (*UR* 15).[9]

As a consequence – he went on to explain – in order to preserve the fullness of the Christian tradition and to bring to a conclusion the reconciliation of Christians of the East and West it is of great importance to preserve and sustain the very rich patrimony of the Eastern Churches, not only for what refers to spiritual and liturgical traditions but also canonical disciplines sanctioned by the Fathers and Councils.

Francis understands that these principles are the essential and reciprocal condition for re-establishing full communion, 'that does not mean either submission of one to the other, or absorption, but rather the acceptance of all the gifts that God has given each in order to manifest to the whole world the great mystery of salvation wrought by Christ the Lord by means of the Holy Spirit.' In these terms he has been working at cultivating a special friendship with Patriarch Bartholomew.

As we have already said, the Patriarch of Constantinople asked to take part in the opening ceremony of Francis' pontificate, an unequivocal sign of the desire to maintain the brotherly relationship begun with the historic embrace between Paul VI and Athenagoras in Jerusalem, when the Second Vatican Council had not yet concluded. Let us look at the preparations that led to the joint celebration of an ecumenical anniversary.

---

9 Cf. Divine Liturgy, address of Pope Francis, Patriarchal Church of St. George, Istanbul Sunday, 30 November 2014, Vatican website under 'Apostolic journeys outside Italy' for 2014.

On the occasion of the feast of Sts Peter and Paul, 29 June 2013, a delegation from the Patriarchate visited the Eternal City. This continued a custom of exchange of delegations between the Church of Constantinople and the Church of Rome begun in 1969. This is how Francis recalled it in during the audience he granted them that evening. In his address he reminded them that 'fraternal encounter is an essential part of the journey to unity.'[10]

In the search for full communion between Catholics and Orthodox, a fundamental work is carried out by the mixed International Commission for Theological Dialogue, co-presided over by Metropolitan John Zizoulas and Cardinal Kurt Koch. Francis underscored the results of years of work, referring in particular to the study of the theological and ecclesiological relationship between primary and collegiality, which saw a basic result in the Ravenna Document (2007).[11]

It is no mere theoretical exercise we are talking about, but a major understanding and knowledge of the peculiarities of each of the traditions: the Catholic Church insists on episcopal collegiality, while the Orthodox Churches insist on synodality. Thanks to the ecumenical journey, these reflections are producing a deep understanding of the ministry of Peter's successor.

10   Cf. Address of His Holiness Pope Francis to the Delegation of the Ecumenical Patriarchate of Constantinople, 28 June, 2013, on Vatican website under 'Addresses' for 2013.
11   Cf. P CODA, *Intercambio de dones: Iglesia católica e Iglesias orientales. El significado estratégico del Documento de Rávena*, in A SPADARO – CM GALLI (eds.), *La reforma y las reformas en la Iglesia*, Sal Terrae, Santander 2016, 425-441. Also available in English in *Reforms of the Church. Reform in the Church*, Paulist Press 2017.

The Pope called attention to the fact that Orthodox and Catholics share the same idea of dialogue which does not seek a minimalist theology of compromise but which 'is based on a deeper understanding of the one truth Christ gave his Church and which we never cease to understand better when moved by the Holy Spirit.' He concluded: 'We need not fear encounter and true dialogue.'

Closer to the feast of St Andrew, 25 November 2013, Francis sent a message to Patriarch Bartholomew through Cardinal Koch, who led the Pontifical delegation which went to Constantinople to take part in the Orthodox Celebrations.[12] The message opened with a quote from the Letter to the Ephesians (6: 23) and began by recalling the journey of the delegation from the Patriarchate which visited Rome during celebrations for Sts Peter and Paul. It is the first time the Pope addressed the Patriarch on the feast of St Andrew, so the message took up the theme of continuing 'fraternal relations between the Churches of Rome and the Ecumenical Patriarchate.'

The God of peace and love has been present in the ecumenical journey of Catholics and Orthodox, making them more aware that we all belong to God 'through the gift of the good news of salvation handed down by the apostles, through the one baptism in the name of the Holy Trinity and through the sacred ministry.' In the light of sharing in this spiritual and theological patrimony we experience the joy of being, and feeling that we are brothers in Christ, although

---

12   AAS 105 (2013) 1170-1172. Cf. R BURIGANA, *Un cuore solo*, 87-90.

there are still obstacles which prevent full communion. We are called to prepare ourselves daily 'through prayer, interior conversion, renewal of life and fraternal dialogue for the moment when we can share together in the Eucharistic celebration.'

A few weeks later, at the *Angelus* on 5 January 2014, Francis made public his decision to make a pilgrimage to the Holy Land from 21-26 May, with three stopovers: Amman, Bethlehem and Jerusalem, to commemorate the historic encounter between Paul VI and Athenagoras.[13]

## 3. *The pilgrimage to the Holy Land: the Common Declaration of Jerusalem*

Francis made use of the general audience on 28 May to offer an overall assessment of his pilgrimage to the Holy Land, the place of historical presence of Christ and the backdrop for fundamental events for Judaism, Christianity and Islam. The principal objective of the trip was to commemorate the meeting of Paul VI and the Patriarch of Constantinople, 'a milestone along the painful yet promising path to Christian unity.'[14] Therefore, he explained, the culminating moment of the pilgrimage was the meeting with Patriarch Bartholomew: they prayed together at the Holy Sepulchre. In that ecumenical prayer in which the Greek Orthodox Patriarch of Jerusalem, Theophilus III, and Armenian Patriarch Apostolic Nourhan Manoughian took

13   Cf. Angelus for 5 January 2014, on Vatican website under 'Angelus – Regina Coeli' for 2014..

14   Cf. *Iter apostolicum in Loca Sancta*: AAS 106 (2014) 456-469; cf. also Vatican website under 'Audiences' for 28 May 2014.

part, along with bishops and pastors of many other Christian communities in the Holy Land, Francis said he 'had felt all the bitterness and suffering of the divisions that still exist between the disciples of Christ.' But he had also been able to feel the desire to heal the wounds and continue tenaciously on the path to full communion. As his predecessors did in years gone by, Bergoglio once again begged 'forgiveness for what we have done to foster this division' and asked 'the Holy Spirit to help us heal the wounds we have caused other brothers.'[15] Together with Bartholomew he shared the willingness to journey together as brothers, pray together, work together for the people of God, seek peace, preserve creation.

This pilgrimage had two other objectives: to encourage the way of peace in that region of the Middle East so rocked by wars and to confirm Christian communities suffering so much in their faith. Nevertheless, we can say that the main thread running through the meeting, words and gestures of Francis' visit to the Holy Land was ecumenism, which reached its peak at the ecumenical celebration at the Holy Sepulchre on Sunday 25 May. This celebration was preceded by the signing of a Common Declaration by the Pope and Patriarch Bartholomew at the Apostolic Delegation in Jerusalem after a private meeting.

This *Declaration*, which has joined the tradition of documents underwritten by Rome and Constantinople, begins by referring to the communique of Paul VI and

---

15   Cf. General Audience on 28 May 2014, as above. R BURIGANA, *Un cuore solo*, 115-129

Athenagoras in 1964. For Francis and Bartholomew, 'this new meeting of the Bishops of the Churches of Rome and Constantinople, founded by the Apostles Peter and Andrew respectively, is the source of a profound spiritual joy.'[16] The meeting provided the opportunity to reflect on the depth and authenticity of existing links, fruit of the path trodden over the last fifty years. This meeting was a new step toward unity realized thanks to the presence and assistance of the Holy Spirit, who leads Christians 'to communion in legitimate diversity.' It is important to observe the wording employed in the *Declaration* to express the model of unity toward which Christians must journey. It is a communion in which the diversity of traditions can and must co-exist. They are differences which have been appearing within Christianity throughout history.

With the meeting of Paul VI and Athenagoras, a silence of centuries was broken and their embrace lifted the mutual excommunication of 1054. This meeting was prolonged by visits between both sees, regular correspondence, and theological dialogue between Catholics and Orthodox begun through the initiative of John Paul II and Patriarch Dimitrios. Over the course of these years, God, 'who is the source of peace and love, has taught us to consider ourselves as members of the same Christian family beneath one only Lord and Saviour Jesus Christ, and to love one another so we can profess our faith in the same gospel of Christ as was received by the Apostles and expressed and passed on to

16  Cf. Vatican website under 'Speeches', 25 May 2014.

us by the Ecumenical Councils and by the Fathers of the Church.' We have not yet achieved full communion, but the authentic aim is to continue journeying together toward the unity for which Christ prayed to the Father 'That they may all be one' (Jn 17:21).

This aim remains tied to Eucharistic celebration, sharing in the Eucharistic banquet. As Christians we are called to prepare ourselves to receive the gift of Eucharistic Communion according to the teaching of Ireneus of Lyon: 'through the profession of the one faith, constant prayer, interior conversion, renewal of life and fraternal dialogue.'[17]

To achieve the objective of full communion, the work of the Mixed Commission of Catholics and Orthodox is essential for theological questions that remain open. This work of theological dialogue is no mere theoretical exercise, but 'an exercise in truth and love which always requires a profound knowledge of each of the two traditions to understand and learn about them.' Finally, the *Declaration* states that the aim of theological dialogue is not to achieve the lowest common denominator which serves to establish a compromise, but that it is about understanding in depth the whole truth that Christ has given his Church. Therefore, fraternal encounter and true dialogue. Through this exchange of gifts the Holy Spirit will guide us to the full truth.

We will close this cycle of the journey taken jointly by Rome and Constantinople to commemorate the ecumenical anniversary 1964-2014 with its prolongation in a second

---

17  *Adversus haereses*, IV, 18, 5.

*Common Declaration* by Francis and Bartholomew I, signed in Istanbul on 30 November, feast of St Andrew. They said that we cannot resign ourselves to a Middle East without Christians. At the same time they took note of the ecumenism of suffering, the ecumenism of blood and martyrdom which so many Christians persecuted in Iraq, Syria and the Middle East are undergoing.[18]

Apart from this and meanwhile, the exchange of ambassadors has continued between Rome and Constantinople for the festivities of Sts Peter and Paul and St Andrew. Other gestures can be added to this: in relation to Francis' Encyclical *Laudate Si'* on looking after our common home (24 May 2015), the Catholic Church has begun to celebrate the day of prayer for the preservation of creation, fixed for the 1$^{st}$ of September. Thus Francis took up once more a practice of the Orthodox Church which celebrates the beginning of the Liturgical Year on that day, the day of Creation.

The dialogue between Rome and Constantinople inevitably affects relations between Rome and Moscow. Rivalry and tensions between the Patriarchates of Constantinople and Moscow are well known. It is a thorny question that we will leave out of our consideration. What we are interested in mentioning is the historic meeting of Francis with Patriarch Kiril of the Russian Orthodox Church at the airport at Havana on 12 February 2016, where

---

[18] Cf. AAS 106 (2014) 967-969; cf also Vatican website, under 'Speeches' for 2014, Ecumenical Blessing and Signing of the Common Declaration, Istanbul, 30 November 2014.

they signed a Common Declaration.[19] Few had believed this meeting possible. Both John Paul II and Benedict XVI had failed in their intent. This meeting in Cuba demonstrated that Pope Francis wants to advance ecumenism through personal encounters that help avoid misunderstandings and overcome prejudices.

## 4. Francis and the Reformation World

To pick up the story again from where we left off, it is worth recalling Francis' words to the plenary meeting of the Pontifical Council for the Promotion of Christian Unity on 20 November 2014.[20] That meeting coincided with the fiftieth anniversary of the promulgation of three documents which encompass the ecclesiological vision of the Second Vatican Council: The Dogmatic Constitution on the Church, *Lumen Gentium*, the Decree on Oriental Catholic Churches, *Orientalium Ecclesiarum*, and the Decree on Ecumenism, *Unitatis Redintegratio*. The five decades following have left behind, as something belonging to the past, the hostility and indifference shown toward other Churches and Ecclesial Communities and this has begun a process of healing which allows us to welcome others as brothers and sisters in the deep unity that comes of baptism.

While giving thanks to God, we must recognize that division among Christians continues, and that differences have appeared over new ethical and anthropological issues

---

19    Cf. AAS 108 (2016) 209-216. On the preparations, R BURIGANA, *Un cuore solo*, 91-93.

20    Cf. AAS 106 (2014) 986-988.

that make the path to unity more complicated. However, we must not yield to resignation but need to continue trusting in God in order to tackle the ecumenical goals today with renewed courage, by cultivating spiritual ecumenism, recognizing the value of the ecumenism of blood, and by journeying together in the way of the gospel. It is worth reflecting on Francis' description of spiritual ecumenism:

> It is a worldwide network of opportunities for prayer which, at the parish and international level, spreads the oxygen of genuine ecumenical spirit through the body of the Church; a network of gestures that unites us by working together in so many works of charity. It is also a sharing of prayer, meditation and other texts which circulate on the Web and can contribute to the growth of knowledge, respect and mutual esteem.[21]

Fifty years after the Decree *Unitatis Redintegratis* – Francis concludes – 'the search for full Christian unity continues to be a priority of the Catholic Church, and for me one of my main daily concerns.'

As already indicated above, the Catholic Church's relationship with Churches and Ecclesial Communities resulting from the 16th century Reformation was influenced by many and complex aspects of an historical and doctrinal nature. The Decree on Ecumenism noted discrepancies affecting the interpretation of revealed truth (*UR* 19),

---

21   *Ibid.*, 987.

which concerns the doctrine regarding Jesus Christ and Redemption, the relationship between Scripture and the Church, authentic magisterium, the Church and its ministries, the role of the Virgin Mary in the work of Redemption (*UR* 20; cf. *USS* 66). The differences are more marked in Eucharistic ecclesiology. To this effect the Decree says that the Ecclesial Communities which arose due to the Reformation have not retained the proper reality of the Eucharistic mystery in its fullness, especially because of the absence of the sacrament of Orders' (*UR* 22).

Certainly, a deeper communion has come about through documents of the Ecumenical Council of Churches, such as *Baptism, Eucharist, Ministry* (1982), texts produced within the Mixed International Anglican–Catholic Commission such as *The gift of authority* (1998) or agreements with the World Lutheran Federation such as the *Joint Declaration on the doctrine of Justification* (1999).[22]

At the beginning of his pontificate, Francis held a meeting with Justin Welby, Archbishop of Canterbury and Primate of the Anglican Communion.[23] Shortly afterwards, on 21 October 2013, he received the delegation from the World Lutheran Federation and members of the Commission for Lutheran–Catholic unity. Among others, the committee included Bishop Munib Younan and Pastor Martin Junge, President and Secretary of the World Lutheran Federation respectively. At that meeting, the

---

22    Cf. W Kasper, *Cosechar los frutos. Aspectos básicos de la fe cristiana en el diálogo ecuménico*, Sal Terrae, Santander 2010.

23    Cf. R Burigana, *Un cuore solo*, 60-65.

Pope began by giving thanks for the steps that Catholics and Protestants have taken in building the visible unity of the Church of Christ.[24] These steps were made concrete in signed agreements, theological dialogue, daily collaboration, as also in a deeper understanding of spiritual ecumenism. Francis alluded to the publication of an important document drawn up in 2013, aimed at the preparation and ecumenical commemoration of the Fifth Centenary of the Protestant Reformation:[25] *From Conflict to Communion: The Lutheran-Catholic Interpretation of the Reformation in 2017*.

All continue to have a vivid memory of Benedict XVI's visit to Germany and the monastery at Erfurt where Luther lived and taught. No surprise, therefore, that Francis would take up some of the Pope Emeritus' words in his own address, to invite patience, dialogue, mutual understanding, knowing full well that unity is not the result of human effort but the action of the Holy Spirit. To end his address Francis had recourse to a quote from the Encyclical *Ut Unum Sint* which speaks of the centrality of reconciliation between Christians in the evangelizing mission of the Church (no. 98).

It is worth rescuing from oblivion the meeting Francis had on 7 March 2014 with the delegation from the Ecumenical Council of Churches, headed by its Secretary General, a

---

24   Cf. AAS 105 (2013) 970-971.
25   Cf. LUTHERAN-ROMAN CATHOLIC COMMISSION ON UNITY, From Conflict to Communion. *Lutheran-Catholic Common Commemoration of the Reformation in 2017*, http://www.vatican.va/roman_curia/pontifical_councils/chrstuni/lutheran-fed-docs/rc_pc_chrstuni_doc_2013_dal-conflitto-alla-comunione_en.html

Lutheran pastor from Norway, Olaf Fyske Tveit.[26] In his address, the Bishop of Rome recognised that since it began, 'the Ecumenical Council of Churches has contributed to shaping the sensitivity of all Christians, making them aware that our divisions are a serious obstacle to the witness of the gospel in the world. These divisions cannot be accepted resignedly as if they were simply an inevitable component of the Church's historical experience.'

Since the Second Vatican Council, the Catholic Church and the Ecumenical Council of Churches have been developing an intense and sincere collaboration, overcoming mutual misunderstanding, making progress in a growing 'exchange of gifts' between the different communities. Francis added: 'the way to full and visible communion is a journey that is arduous still today, but on the move.' Without doubt, the document *The Church: Toward a Common Vision*, presented during the last general assembly of the Ecumenical Council of Churches held in Busan (South Korea, 30 October to 8 November 2013) will be decisive for the future progress of the ecumenical movement.

More recently, on 23 June 2015, commemorating the fiftieth anniversary of collaboration between the Catholic Church and the Ecumenical Council of Churches, the Pope stressed the fact that it had produced an intense collaboration not only in ecumenical matters but also in the field of inter-religious dialogue, peace and social justice, the work of charity and humanitarian aid. This way he was

26    Cf. Vatican website under 'Speeches' for 7 March 2014.

returning to one of his famous principles: 'reality is more important than the idea.'[27]

In 2006, the World Methodist Council expressed its adherence to the *Joint Declaration on Justification* agreed on previously by Lutherans and Catholics. An audience granted a Methodist delegation on 7 April 2016 took place under these auspices. On that occasion Francis offered a quote from the Letter to a Roman Catholic by John Wesley: 'Though we are not able to think about things yet in the same way, we can still love in the same way.'[28]

These meetings with the Anglican Communion, the World Lutheran Federation and the Ecumenical Council of Churches and many others we have not looked at, convince us of Francis' deep interest in pursuing the ecumenical journey without ignoring current difficulties.

## 5. *The opportunity offered by the Fifth Centenary of the Lutheran Reformation: the Pope's trip to Sweden*

An ecumenical celebration took place on 31 October 2016, to commemorate the origins of the Protestant Reformation. Bishop Munib Youan, President of the World Lutheran Federation, and Secretary, Pastor Martin Junge, had invited the Churches to come together in the Swedish city where the Federation came into being in 1947. He also invited the Bishop of Rome. We are faced with an extraordinary event. Never until now had a pope been invited

27  Cf. AAS 107 (2015) 643-644.
28  Cf. AAS 108 (2016) 549-550. Recently announced (5 July 2017), adherence of the Communion of Reformed Churches to the Joint Declaration on Justification (1999).

to a commemoration of the Lutheran Reform. Without doubt, the Pope's trip to Sweden is the result of fifty years of dialogue between Catholics and Lutherans. That day, in the Romanesque Cathedral in Lund, a chain of events began which focused precisely on this symbolic date of 31 October 2017, the day of celebration of the Reformation's fifth centenary. Let us go back over the preparations.

On 4 May 2015, Antje Jackelen, the female Archbishop of Upsala, visited Rome together with a delegation from the Evangelical Lutheran Church of Sweden. 'Catholics and Lutherans' Francis said, 'have to seek and promote unity in diocese, parishes and communities around the world.'[29] As well as recalling the earlier-mentioned text, *From Conflict to Community*, he was grateful for the help that the Swedish Lutheran Church had given to many South American immigrants during the time of the dictatorship; and in a personal way, he thanked them for the mention of Pastor Ruuth, with whom Bergoglio had shared the Chair of Spiritual Theology and who had helped him so much in his spiritual life.

Some months later, on 15 November, Francis visited the Evangelical and Lutheran Church in Rome. There he replied spontaneously to questions from the members of that community.[30] As, for example, a woman married to a Roman Catholic who expressed her sorrow at 'not being

29    Francisco, *Discurso a la señora Antje Jackelén, arzobispo de Upsala, y a una delegación de la Iglesia evangélica luterana de Suecia*, online: www.vatican.va, 4 May 2015.
30    Francisco, *Visita a la Iglesia evangélica y luterana de Roma. Discurso*, online: www.vatican.va, 15 November 2015.

able to share the Lord's Supper.' His brief homily ended with a statement and a plea. 'Today we have prayed together and we will seek to work together for the poor, the needy. Let us love one another with true brotherly love.' The prayer alluded to theologian Oscar Cullmann who spoke 'of the hour of reconciled diversity'; 'Let us ask for this grace today, the grace of this reconciled diversity in the Lord.'

During the press conference which took place on the return flight from the apostolic journey to Armenia on 26 June 2016, a journalist asked him about his imminent trip to Sweden and a possible rehabilitation of Luther. This is how he replied:[31]

> I believe Martin Luther's intentions were not mistaken; he was a reformer. Perhaps some approaches were not appropriate, but at that time… the Church was not exactly a model to be imitated. There was corruption, worldliness, attachment to money and power in the Church. This is what he protested against… And today, Lutherans and Catholics, together with all Protestants, are in agreement on the doctrine of justification. Today it is about us resuming the journey to meet with one another after 500 years. I believe we must pray together and secondly, work for the poor, the persecuted, for so many people who suffer… Work together and pray

---

31   Press Conference on return trip from Armenia, www.vatican.va, 26 June 2016

together. May theologians study together, seeking. It is a long, very long journey.

Again, the ecumenism of mercy and doctrinal dialogue. Francis' apostolic trip to Sweden lasted two days, from 31 October to 1 November. Initially, Mass with Swedish Catholics was not on the agenda, given that before anything else the visit was an 'ecumenical witness.' However, Francis admitted[32] that he thought better of it, and after the fervent request of the Catholic community, he decided to celebrate a Mass at Malmö. That is what happened, and on 31 October, a joint ecumenical prayer service took place in the Lutheran Cathedral in Lund and on All Saints Day he celebrated the Eucharist for Swedish Catholics and those from neighbouring countries like Norway and Denmark.

The ecumenical liturgy in Lund Cathedral focused on the Gospel passage 'remain in me and I in you' (Jn 15:4). 'Catholics and Lutherans are committed to walking together on the journey to reconciliation.' He added:[33]

> Now, in the context of the Common Commemoration of the Reformation in 1517 we have a new opportunity for accepting a common journey that has been taking shape over the last fifty years in the ecumenical dialogue between the World Lutheran Federation and the Catholic Church. We have the opportunity to mend a crucial moment in

32  Cf. U Jonsson, *Intervista a Papa Francesco*, 323.
33  *Viaje apostólico a Suecia. Homilía del Santo Padre*, www.vatican.va, 31 October 2016

our history by overcoming controversies and misunderstandings that have often hindered us from understanding one another.

God is the owner of the vineyard and we have to remain as living branches united with his Son Jesus Christ. With gratitude he recognized that the Reformation had contributed to placing great focus on the Holy Scriptures in the life of the Church. His Word keeps us united. Finally, Francis reminded them that 'Martin Luther's spiritual experience challenges us and reminds us that we can do nothing without God.' The question he constantly pursued: 'How can I have a merciful God?' presents the question of our right relationship with God, which is the decisive question in human life. Luther encountered this merciful God in the Good News of Jesus Christ who became man, died and rose again. His principle, 'by divine grace alone' expresses the initiative of God who precedes any human response in such a way that the doctrine of justification contains the essence of human existence before God.

At the end of the prayer, the President of the World Lutheran Federation and the Pope signed a *Joint Declaration* as part of the Catholic-Lutheran commemoration of the Reformation:

> Our common faith in Jesus Christ and our baptism demand an ongoing conversion of us in order to leave behind the historical disagreements and conflicts which obstruct the ministry of reconciliation. While the past cannot be changed for what we remember and

how we remember it, it can be transformed.
Let us pray for a healing of our wounds and
memory.

## 6. Summary. We are pilgrims and we are on pilgrimage together: peace is an art

At the conclusion of this twofold journey focused on Francis' pilgrimage to the Holy Land and his trip to Sweden as a reflection of the process of reunification of East and West and Catholic-Protestant ecumenism, we can conclude with Bruigana that the Pope's gestures and words entail a relaunching and strengthening of the ecumenical dialogue that was showing signs of resignation, distrust and slowing down.[34] The ecumenical spirit of Francis remains focused on the main idea that is picked up by the title of this chapter: journeying together. Hence, this journey forms part of the horizon of full communion between Christians, a long and arduous journey where speaking, praying, and working together for unity relies ultimately on trust in the promise made to Abraham: 'Go to the land that I will give you.'

His understanding and practice of ecumenism is well summed up in the message he addressed to Evangelical Christians at Caserta, an Evangelical Pentecostal Community, during a private visit on 28 July 2014. At that gathering he sought to pas on the following thought; 'The Spirit creates diversity but also unity.'[35]

---

34 R BURIGANA, *Un cuore solo*, 131.
35 Cf. Vatican website under 'Speeches' for 28 July 2014.

Bergoglio picked up the idea proposed by the Evangelical pastor: our Christian life is 'walking' in the presence of the Lord Jesus. The Christian must continue to walk on bravely, with *parresia*, with hope: 'Inert Christians – this does harm, because what doesn't move doesn't work, becomes corrupted; like stagnant water...' For this journey, he gives us his Spirit. According to Chapter 12 of the First Letter to the Corinthians, the Spirit creates 'diversity' in the Church. However, the same Spirit creates unity, so the Church is one in diversity. Without mentioning his name, Francis evoked "*an evangelical whom I love*" – O Cullmann – who speaks of a 'reconciled diversity' through the Holy Spirit. The Spirit creates diversity out of charisms and the Spirit is also the author of harmony among charisms. This is why the Fathers of the Church said that the Holy Spirit is harmony.

We are living at a time of globalization. What will Church unity look like, and what is globalization? Francis rejects the idea that we must think in terms of the sphere as our norm, meaning that all points are equal and equidistant from the centre. No. That is uniformity, but the Holy Spirit does not create uniformity. This is why we need to think of the geometric figure of the polyhedron: 'the polyhedron is a unity but of all different parts; each has its peculiarity, its charism. It is unity in diversity.' This way we can understand what 'ecumenism' means theologically: it is about 'this diversity being more harmonized by the Holy Spirit and achieving unity.' This is what it means to walk in God's presence, to meet up with our brothers and sisters.

In his Apostolic Exhortation, *Evangelii Gaudium*, which we will analyze in the next chapter, we read the same idea through the prism of 'we are pilgrims journeying alongside one another (*EG* 244). Francis places the emphasis on a very wise condition: 'We must have sincere trust in our fellow pilgrims, putting aside all suspicion or mistrust, and turn our gaze to what we are all seeking: the radiant peace of God's face. Trusting others is an art and peace is an art. Jesus told us: "Blessed are the peacemakers" (Mt 5: 9).'

## Chapter 4
## FRANCIS' ECUMENICAL PROGRAM: RE-READING *EVANGELII GAUDIUM*

As we have begun to see, Francis places special emphasis on the dialogue of charity, concern for friendship and human relationships. It is a very important dimension, which is soundly sustained by spiritual ecumenism, the heart of which is prayer and personal conversion. Francis has made us feel the impatience once more for unity through his own manner and style. He knows that at times, theological dialogues are very difficult, but they cannot be done without. We have been providing evidence of his general approach to the great questions of the ecumenical agenda as we find them in his words and deeds, his gestures and texts, even casual remarks at times. Now we will attempt to distil the underlying theology of his ecumenical vision running through the major text of his magisterium, *Evangelii Gaudium*, his Apostolic Exhortation of an agenda-setting nature,[1] published on 24 November 2013. But first, some preliminary observations.

### 1. *Methodological preamble: keys for interpretation*

There are only three numbers in the Apostolic Exhortation *Evangelii Gaudium* dedicated to ecumenism

1   Cf. *EG* 25. S MADRIGAL, *La «Iglesia en salida»: la misión como tema eclesiológico*, in *Revista Catalana de Teología* 40/2 (2015) 425-458.

(cf. *EG* 244-246) which take account in their brevity of the principal propositions of the Decree on Ecumenism *Unitatis Redintegratio* of the Second Vatican Council. The text recalls that 'the credibility of the Christian message would be much greater if Christians could overcome their divisions and the Church could realize 'the fullness of catholicity proper to her in those of her children who, though joined to her by baptism, are yet separated from full communion with her" (*EG* 244; Cf. *UR* 4). The Pope expresses his confidence in being able to 'progress decidedly towards common expressions of proclamation, service and witness,' from the principle of the *hierarchy of truths* (*EG* 246). Besides, he recognizes the importance of an *exchange of gifts* which helps us to progress toward truth and good, as John Paul II taught us in *Ut Unum Sint*.[2]

However, we cannot say that we have exhausted the problem here relating to the search for church unity. As we have already indicated, ecumenism for Francis is a way of living Christianity. He confirms this first observation by presenting these three paragraphs not as isolated fragments but as part of a section dedicated to 'social dialogue,' meaning that ecumenism is presented as a form of *dialogue* along with following other approaches: dialogue between faith, reason and science (242-243), relations with Judaism (247-249) and inter-religious dialogue (250-254), social dialogue in a context of religious freedom (255-258).

2   See: 'Condividere i doni. *L'esortazione post-sinodale 'Evangelii gaudium'*, in R Burigana, *Un cuore solo*, 73-82. Cf. V Fernández – P Rodari, *La Iglesia del Papa Francisco*, 151-152 (Cf. *The Francis Project* … ).

A second observation: it is important to note that this section on 'Social Dialogue as a contribution to peace' comes at the end of an extensive Chapter 4 whose overall theme is 'The social dimension of evangelization' with two main sub-themes: social inclusion of the poor and the common good and peace in society. The gospel of mercy with its inherent social involvement must prevail over 'the globalization of indifference.'

To that we add a third consideration: the content of the section on the common good and peace in society (217-237) which comes before the section on dialogue in general and ecumenical dialogue in particular, is none other than the four principles set out by the Cardinal of Buenos Aires for establishing a political culture which has encounter rather than confrontation as its aim: time is greater than space, unity prevails over conflict, realities are more important than ideas, the whole is greater than the part. Therefore the same principles which inspire political action and building up peace in society and between nations inspire theological and pastoral action and are applicable to the People of God and ecumenical relations between Churches. Becoming a people is 'a slow and arduous effort calling for a desire for integration and a willingness to achieve this through the growth of a peaceful and multifaceted culture of encounter' (*EG* 220). In fact we have noticed in the preceding chapter that the Argentinian Pope used these 'priorities' in his ecumenical reflections.

In other words: Francis is a systematic thinker and this means that the key ideas of his ecumenical program can be glimpsed within the basic core of his pastoral, theological, philosophical and political program with its substance in the proclamation of the gospel of mercy and peace (Eph 6:15)[3]. 'In this perspective, ecumenism can be seen as a contribution to the unity of the human family' (*EG* 245). This being the case, ecumenical dialogue is at the heart of his program for reforming the Church.

The Church cannot wash its hands of the serious questions of human rights, the very poor, and protection of our common home. In beautiful, brief strokes he described the Church's evangelizing activity as 'Small yet strong in the love of God, like Saint Francis of Assisi, all of us, as Christians, are called to watch over and protect the fragile world in which we live, and all its peoples' (*EG* 216). As a consequence, to capture the ecumenical vision of the Pope in all its depth it is necessary to explore more deeply his agenda-setting text.

He himself has given us some leads. Right from the outset, in the first chapter, he referred to the hierarchy of truths (*EG* 36). In the second chapter, when he analyzes the signs of the times today, he opens his reflection with the title 'No to warring among ourselves' (*EG* 98-101) which considers precisely the fact of so many wars caused by envy and jealousy, even among Christians (*EG* 98) and the fact that old divisions and conflicts are re-emerging. Hence he asks for the witness of fraternal communion, appealing to the Johannine passage of the priestly prayer where Jesus

3   Cf. W Thönissen, *Papst Franziskus und die Ökumene*, in *Catholica* (M) 70 (2016) 57-77; here: 73.

prays for unity 'That they may all be one… in us… so that the world may believe' (*EG* 99). He does so again in the third chapter when he deals with the evangelizing People of God and formulates the thesis of unity and diversity, the work of the Holy Spirit, the true 'guide' of evangelization:

> Differences between persons and communities can sometimes prove uncomfortable, but the Holy Spirit, who is the source of that diversity, can bring forth something good from all things and turn it into an attractive means of evangelization. Diversity must always be reconciled by the help of the Holy Spirit; he alone can raise up diversity, plurality and multiplicity while at the same time bringing about unity. When we, for our part, aspire to diversity, we become self-enclosed, exclusive and divisive; similarly, whenever we attempt to create unity on the basis of our human calculations, we end up imposing a monolithic uniformity. This is not helpful for the Church's mission (*EG* 131).

This analysis anticipates the typically Bergoglian way of approaching the ecumenical problem: unity through reconciled diversity in the Holy Spirit. In the light of these guidelines we will undertake a re-reading of *Evangelii Gaudium* which moves through the following steps: a) We have to begin from the heart of the gospel, taking into consideration the hierarchy of truths; b) Since God's primary and principal characteristic is mercy, we need to overcome conflicts and seek unity through reconciliation of our doctrinal differences in a climate of readiness to forgive; c) So we can learn from one another, making progress on the ecumenical journey through an exchange of gifts.

## 2. *The heart of the gospel and the hierarchy of truths*

The Apostolic Exhortation is the result of the 13th Ordinary Assembly of the Synod of Bishops held from 7-28 October 2012, whose theme was 'The new evangelization for the transmission of the Faith.'[4] Present were the Patriarch of Constantinople Bartholomew I and the then Archbishop of Canterbury, Rowan D. Williams.

The first chapter of *Evangelii Gandium* is dedicated to the missionary transformation of the Church. For Francis, the key to renewal is to attend to the mission, overcome ecclesial introversion. At the beginning of the Apostolic Exhortation we read that 'missionary outreach is paradigmatic for all the Church's activity' (*EG* 15). This was the conviction of the Latin American Bishops gathered at Aparecida (2007) and the Exhortation *Evangelii Gaudium* echoes it: It is necessary to move 'from pastoral ministry of mere conservation to a decidedly missionary pastoral ministry' (*DA* 370; quoted in *EG* 15). The program of a 'Church which goes forth' finds substance in 'missionary conversion for reform of the Church.' Elsewhere he confesses he wrote this document to encourage members of the Church in a 'process of missionary reform' (*LS* 3).

---

4   Cf. HM YÁÑEZ (ed.), *Evangelii gaudium: il testo ci interroga. Chiavi di lettura, testimonianze e prospettive*, Gregorian & Biblical Press, Rome 2014.

Francis speaks, at the beginning, of 'the delightful and comforting joy of evangelizing' (*EG* 9-10). Everything flows from this. In fact this statement is taken from paragraph 80 of Blessed Paul VI's Apostolic Exhortation *Evangelii Nuntiandi* (1975) a document to which the current Pope attributes exceptional importance. We know that when Aparecida Document (2007) was being finally drafted, the Cardinal of Buenos Aires asked that this sentence be included in the text of conclusions at the end.[5]

The renewal of an outgoing Church must come from the heart of the gospel (*EG* 34-39). We have to go to the roots, to the heart of the gospel: 'In this basic core, what shines forth is the beauty of the saving love of God made manifest in Jesus Christ who died and rose from the dead' (*EG* 36). Our reflection on evangelization must begin from the principle of the primacy of grace (cf. *EG* 12). Therefore it is the novelty of the gospel which must breathe fresh air into the Church's mission and also ecumenism.

In this context, Francis takes up once more a teaching of the Second Vatican Council that is one of his favourite themes:[6] 'in Catholic doctrine there exists an order or a 'hierarchy' of truths, since they vary in their relation to the foundation of the Christian faith' (*EG* 36; cf. *UR* 11). Theologians like Rahner or Cullmann considered this statement to be one of the most important discussions of

5 Cf. S MADRIGAL, *El giro eclesiológico en la recepción del Vaticano II*, 295-296.

6 Cf. V FERNÁNDEZ – P RODARI, *La Iglesia del Papa Francisco*, 55-61 (*The Francis Project* … ). EJ ECHEVERRÍA, *El Papa Francisco. El legado del Vaticano II*, Desclée de Brouwer, Bilbao 2017, 255-265.

Vatican II for the future of ecumenical theology, which should help to better understand what unites and divides us Christians in doctrinal matters.

This principle, which also applies to dogmas of the faith and moral teaching, states that there is an order or hierarchy between truths that comes from their different relationships with the foundation of the Christian faith, meaning faith in God who is one and three in the Incarnation of the Son of God, our Redeemer. Just as no virtue can be excluded from the Christian ideal, so no particular truth can be denied, which would deform the integrity of the gospel message. Each needs to be considered in its relationship to the heart of the message of Jesus Christ's gospel.

As Kasper has explained, the hierarchy of truths is not a principle for determining which doctrinal truths or divine commands are secondary so as to declare them less binding or optional. There is no such thing. The hierarchy of truths is a hermeneutical principle of an inclusive rather than exclusive nature.[7] This being the case, the hierarchy of truths never means indifference, but the principle implies a systematic and integral vision: some truths are more important for more directly expressing the heart of the gospel, which others do so more indirectly. If all revealed truths come from the same divine source, they have to be believed with the same faith. 'Each truth' Francis explains, 'is better understood when related to the harmonious totality

---

7   Cf. W KASPER, *Die ökumenische Vision von Papst Franziskus*, 25.

of the Christian message; in this context all of the truths are important and illumine one another' (*EG* 39).

Our message must never lose its freshness, that is, its 'fragrance of the gospel.' He has given us a series of guidelines on this in the third chapter of the Exhortation dedicated to the proclamation of the Gospel: 'there can be no true evangelization without the explicit proclamation of Jesus as Lord' (*EG* 110). And elsewhere: 'All evangelization is based on [the word of God], listened to, meditated upon, lived, celebrated and witnessed to. The sacred Scriptures are the very source of evangelization… It is indispensable that the word of God be ever more fully at the heart of every ecclesial activity' (*EG* 174).

Taking the gospel as the point of reference and underlining the fundamental importance of the Sacred Scripture and its kerygmatic proclamation, are elements which must satisfy our ecumenical partners from the evangelical Lutheran and Calvinist traditions. We need to meet with them again on the common ground of the gospel. This is where perhaps the Bergoglian principle comes in which states that the whole is greater than the part:

> To Christians, this principle also evokes the totality or integrity of the Gospel which the Church passes down to us and sends us forth to proclaim… The Gospel has an intrinsic criterion of totality: it will always remain good news until it has been proclaimed to all people, until it has healed and strengthened every aspect of humanity, until it has brought

all men and women together at the table in God's kingdom. The whole is greater than the part (*EG* 237).

In our re-reading of *Evangelii Gandium*, the moment has come for examining the ecumenical repercussions of the Bergoglian principles which sustain the theology of the people.[8]

*3. The model of unity in reconciled diversity: the figure of the polyhedron*

The fundamental goal of ecumenism is Church unity, so therefore we need to work at overcoming historical divisions and new conflicts. Particularly serious is 'the counter-witness of division among Christians, particularly in Asia and Africa,' (*EG* 246) where the search for paths to unity becomes all the more urgent. Coming into effect here is the Bergoglian principle that says 'unity prevails over conflict' (*EG* 226-230) from which flows an illuminating analysis:

> Conflict cannot be ignored or concealed. It has to be faced. But if we remain trapped in conflict, we lose our perspective, our horizons shrink and reality itself begins to fall apart. In the midst of conflict we lose our sense of the profound unity of reality (*EG* 226).

---

8   Cf. W Henn, *Intercambio de dones: la recepción de los frutos del diálogo y la reforma de la Iglesia*, in A Spadaro – CM Galli, *La reforma y las reformas en la Iglesia*, 399-423; here: 401-407 (*Reforms of the Church. Reform in the Church* ... ).

Three possible attitudes are contemplated: those who, when conflict arises, have no desire to tackle it; those who become prisoners of it, making unity impossible; and those who face conflict head on, resolve it (cf. *EG* 227). Only this way when we go beyond the surface conflict and look at others in their deepest dignity does it 'become possible to build community amid disagreement.' Hence the essential principle for building friendship in society: namely, that unity is greater than conflict' (*EG* 228). Solidarity thus becomes a way of making history and is different from syncretism, different from absorption of one by the other. It is about resolution of conflict 'on [a] higher plane and preserves what is valid and useful on both sides.' Christ is the sign of this unity and the reconciliation of all things. In him is peace. 'Christ is our peace' (Eph. 2: 14).

Bergoglio reflected on this in his conversations with Rabbi Skorka. 'The question' he said at the time 'is how one resolves conflict according to the word of God.' His point of view was expressed as follows:

> I believe that the path to resolution should never be war, because that would imply that one of the two poles in tension will absorb the other. Nor is it resolved through a synthesis which is a hybrid mixture of the two extremes, something hybrid with no future. The poles in tension are resolved on a higher plane, looking toward the horizon, not in a synthesis but in a new unity, a new pole that keeps the virtues of both, assumes them and

goes on from there. It is not an absorption or hybrid synthesis, it is a new unity.[9]

A little further on in that conversation he appealed to the technical formula coined by theologian Oscar Cullmann (1902-1999), one of the Protestant observers at the Second Vatican Council: unity is reconciled diversity.[10] As we have noted in the previous chapter, Francis often has recourse to him in the context of the reunification of East and West, but above all for Catholic – Protestant ecumenism.

He enriched this reflection in *Evangelii Gaudium* with another element. The message of peace obeys 'the conviction that the unity brought by the Spirit can harmonize every diversity. It overcomes every conflict by creating a new promising synthesis. Diversity is a beautiful thing when it can constantly enter into a process of reconciliation and seal a sort of cultural covenant resulting in a "reconciled diversity"' (*EG* 230).

Some years ago, Ratzinger expressed his preference for one of Cullmann's formulas, to 'achieve unity *through* diversity,' meaning 'to take what is fruitful in division, detoxify one's division and take from diversity what is positive; naturally in the hope that in the end, the break will rapidly cease to be such and will mean only a "polarity"

---

9   JM BERGOGLIO – A SKORKA, *Sobre el cielo y la tierra*, 200 (*On Heaven and Earth* … ).

10   *Ibid.*, 204. Cf. W KASPER, *El papa Francisco*, 87-88 (*Pope Francis' Revolution of Tenderness and Love* … ). O CULLMANN, *Einheit durch Vielfalt. Grundlegung und Beitrag zur Diskussion über die Möglichkeit ihrer Verwirklichung*, Mohr, Tubingen 1986.

without contradictions.'[11] I think this description fits in well with Francis' proposal for ecumenical activity: seeking full unity by establishing models of unity and by illuminating points of opposition in order to head towards unity. On the other hand, we know that it is not we who bring about unity but the Holy Spirit who is harmony. In a word: we can be also united in our divided situations.

Francis described 'reconciled diversity' as a dynamic process of 'seeking the truth while journeying together in the unity of our baptism in trinitarian communion.' This is spiritual ecumenism. He explains: 'Deepening dialogue to accede more fully to the truth, by exploring our truths in a dialogue that God begins, not us, and that it has its own time and pedagogy. A dialogue that is *a journey toward truth together*.'[12]

The formula of unity through diversity finds graphic expression in the Pope's texts: the model of unity is not the sphere but the polyhedron. We have already seen at the end of the previous chapter, that he used this image during his meeting with the Pentecostal community at Caserta to describe the journey in the common search for unity. His model is not the sphere 'where every point is equidistant from the centre, and there are no differences between them. Instead it is the polyhedron, which reflects the convergence

11   Cf. J RATZINGER, *Iglesia, ecumenismo y política. Nuevos ensayos de eclesiología*, BAC, Madrid 1987, 153-160 here: 157. Also available in English as *Church, Ecumenism and Politics: New Endeavours in Ecclesiology*, Paulist Press, 2008.
12   Cf. JM BERGOGLIO, *Educar, elegir la vida*, Claretianas, Buenos Aires 2015, 62.

of all its parts, each of which preserves its distinctiveness,' and takes 'the best of each' (*EG* 236). Here he shows that unity is not uniformity.

This original and eloquent image, Cardinal Kasper comments, preserves the peculiarity of the different Churches without hiding the identity of the whole.[13] It is clear that diversity is not valued for itself and independently of its relationship with the whole. Certainly, much room is given to the difference and specific nature of each of the distinct Churches. However, for its correct interpretation another Bergoglian principle comes into play: the whole is greater than the part such that the whole is not reduced to being the sum or aggregate of the parts (cf. *EG* 234-237). In any case, it enables an ecumenical process of learning and a complementary relationship of reciprocal enrichment. It is about taking up and recognizing what the Spirit has sowed in them as a gift for us.

We will immediately consider this exchange of gifts or receptive ecumenism. Let us close this section this section with a final observation. This goal of journeying toward full communion through reconciliation of diversity is a long-term one. This is why this ecumenical program brings in a fundamental principle in order to move forward: the priority of time over space. 'This principle allows us to work slowly but surely without being obsessed by immediate results. It helps us patiently to endure difficult and adverse situations, or inevitable changes in our plans... Giving priority to time

---

13  Cf. W Kasper, *El papa Francisco*, 89 (*Pope Francis' Revolution of Tenderness and Love* ... ).

means being concerned about *initiating processes rather than processing spaces*' (*EG* 223). Within the perspective of the call of *Deus semper maior*, he inserts the utopia which opens us to the future as the final cause which attracts us: 'Go to the land I will give you.'

## 4. *The exchange of gifts: receptive ecumenism*

The concept of 'reception' has acquired a double sense in the area of ecumenical theology, as formulated in the Encyclical *Ut Unum Sint*. On the one hand, St John Paul II refers to the important task of receiving the results achieved in ecumenical dialogue, which cannot remain on the desks of bilateral commissions of specialists but need to become part of the common patrimony of the people of God (cf. *UUS* 80). The pages of the Encyclical are a good exponent of this, since in making reference to some important documents like the Lima Document (192) it becomes an example of reception of the results achieved. On the other hand, Pope Wojtyla echoes this other form of acceptance: ecumenical dialogue is always 'an exchange of gifts' (cf. *UUS* 28). In this sense the agreed documents become intermediaries for knowledge and mutual recognition.

This dimension of the ecumenism of the exchange of gifts was recently formalized in the expression 'receptive ecumenism.'[14] Its basic principle can be described thus: ecumenical responsibility must come not from the question

---

14  Cf. PD MURRAY (ed.), *Receptive Ecumenism and the Call to Catholic Learning. Exploring a Way for Contemporary Ecumenism*, Oxford University Press, Oxford-New York 2008.

of what the other traditions should learn from us but another – what we need to learn from them. In other words, ecumenism is an exchange of gifts that makes it possible for the different confessional traditions – Catholic, Protestant and Orthodox – to learn from one another. Francis' statements are situated within this conceptual framework:

> If we really believe in the abundantly free working of the Holy Spirit, we can learn so much from one another! It is not just about being better informed about others, but rather about reaping what the Spirit has sown in them, which is also meant to be a gift for us. To give but one example, in the dialogue with our Orthodox brothers and sisters, we Catholics have the opportunity to learn more about the meaning of episcopal collegiality and their experience of synodality. Through an exchange of gifts, the Spirit can lead us ever more fully into truth and goodness. (*EG* 246).

The text offers us the example of synodality and collegiality practised by the Orthodox Churches. He indicated it as follows in the interview granted Spadaro in August 2013: 'I want to pursue the reflection on how to exercise the Petrine primacy that began with the Mixed Commission in 2007 and which led to the signing of the Ravenna Document. This is the path we need to follow.'[15] The two Declarations

---

15  A. Spadaro Interview with Pope Francis, on Vatican website: w2.vatican.va/content/francesco/en/speeches/2013/september/documents/papa-francesco_20130921_intervista-

signed together by Francis and Bartholomew I in Jerusalem (25 May 2014) and Istanbul (30 November 2014) speak of this exchange of gifts. The primacy–collegiality relationship was a much debated issue during the Second Vatican Council. Francis, who feels that the function of primacy, if it is to be also promoted, challenged and reconfigured the ecumenical encounter, is in need of promoting 'a healthy 'decentralization' (*EG* 16).

Without doubt, the process of centralization of the Catholic Church has been an incentive for resistance of other Christian Communities to seeking full communion with the Bishops of Rome. Francis described the Extraordinary Synod of Bishops as a great experience of synodality and collegiality.[16] This idea of a pastoral conversion of the primacy through the synodal principle has been re-elaborated more systematically in the address he gave on the occasion of the fiftieth anniversary of the institution of the Synod of Bishops on 17 October 2015, suggesting a synodal Church.[17]

Other examples of this exchange of gifts could be offered, beginning with the ancient Syriac, Coptic and Armenian Eastern Churches. The Latin Catholic Church can learn much from the liturgy, spirituality and ecclesiology of the East.[18] As we indicated in the previous chapter, on his

spadaro.html

16   Cf. See Vatican website, under 'Speeches', closing address, 18 October 2014: AAS 106 (2014) 835-839.

17   Cf. AAS 107 (2015) 1138-1144.

18   Cf. J FAMERÉE, *Intercambio de dones: Iglesia católica e Iglesias orientales. Por un consenso diferenciado*, in A SPADARO – CM GALLI, *La reforma y las reformas en la Iglesia*, 443-456 (*Reforms of*

trip to Sweden Francis pointed to two fundamental aspects that Catholics must explore by looking at ourselves in the mirror of the Lutheran tradition: reform and Scripture.[19] On this fifth centenary of the Reformation the Pope asks us to seriously explore the figure of Luther, and his criticism of the Church, of the Church of his day. At the closing of the Octave for Christian Unity with Vespers at St Paul-outside-the-walls on 25 January 2017, he encouraged everyone to continue on the journey of reconciliation and dialogue, to proclaim the gospel in word and deed, to live and give witness to a reconciled existence that God has offered us in Christ. Authentic reconciliation between Christians will come about 'when we know how to recognize the gifts of others and are able to learn from one another with humility and docility, without hoping that it is the other who first learn from us.'

Given that 'Catholic' and 'sectarian' are two words in contradiction, Francis does not exclude anyone in the exchange of gifts, not even Pentecostal groups. The meteoric emergence of these groups has become a disconcerting sign of the times as the most dynamic and vital current of contemporary Christianity, a great challenge for the Catholic Church in many geographical contexts in Latin America. His private meetings with Evangelicals and

*the Church. Reform in the Church* ... ).

19   U Jonsson, *Intervista a Papa Francesco*, 317. P De Mey, *Aprender de medio siglo de diálogo con las Iglesias nacidas de la Reforma. Por la reforma de la Iglesia católica hoy*, in *La reforma y las reformas en la Iglesia*, 457-473.

Pentecostals have not gone unnoticed.[20] These gestures have their antecedents in Bergoglio's performance as Archbishop of Buenos Aires and in the place he assigns to spiritual ecumenism with those Christians with whom it is not possible to establish any other kind of dialogue.

This presents us with a major challenge. Due to the Catholic principle of ecumenism we need to think that 'elements of sanctification and truth' (cf. *LG* 15; *UR* 3) are present in Pentecostal groups in order to draw out the appropriate ecclesiological consequences, in the sense that these groups exhibit a range of elements which, as diffused and dispersed as they seem, are really those of the Church of Christ and lean toward 'the catholic unity' of the Church (*LG* 8).

## 5. Summary. *The Holy Spirit harmonizes and reconciles diversity on the journey toward unity*

Our re-reading of the Apostolic Exhortation, *Evangelii Gaudium*, has highlighted the fact that ecumenical dialogue which is situated within the perspective of a social dialogue in order to achieve the unity of the human family, has deep evangelical roots in the Gospel of mercy which establishes the intimate connections between evangelization and human promotion, and which invites everyone to have a true experience of fraternity, encounter and solidarity. The Gospel, the Pope reminds us, always invites us to run the

---

20  Cf. JA Scampini, *Pentecostales y católicos: Hacia un 'intercambio de dones' para un anuncio renovado del Evangelio*, en *La reforma y las reformas en la Iglesia*, 475-493; here: 480-481.

risk of encountering the other face-to-face: 'True faith in the incarnate Son of God is inseparable from self-giving, from membership in the community, from service, from reconciliation with others. The Son of God, by becoming flesh, summoned us to the revolution of tenderness (*EG* 88). The incarnation is the theological fact on which the Bergoglian principle is based, one we have not as yet taken into consideration: 'Realities are greater than ideas' (*EG* 233). The Christian ideal is inspired by the realism of the social dimension of the gospel which demands ongoing fraternity, this being a specific component of ecclesial mysticism. To conclude, we would like to plumb the theological basis of this ecumenical vision.

1. It is good to recall, in the first instance, that the theme of Church unity already appears in Francis' first Encyclical, *Lumen Fidei*, a text planned by Benedict XVI as a completion of his trilogy on the theological virtues. The Argentinian Pope made it his own (*LF* 7). There we read: 'The unity of the Church, in time and space, is linked to the unity of the faith: "There is one body and one Spirit… one faith (Eph 4:5)"' (*LF* 47). What is the secret of unity of faith? First of all, faith is one through the unity of God; secondly, faith is one because it is addressed to the One Lord, the life and mystery of Jesus Christ, to the history he shared with us; finally, 'faith is one because it is shared by the whole Church which forms one only body and one only spirit.' Therefore 'the unity of faith is the unity of the Church,' such that 'to subtract something from the faith is to subtract something from the veracity of communion' (*LF* 48). This approach

situates us before the theo-christo-ecclesio-logical core of the ecumenical problem with its final objective of achieving full communion.

2. Secondly, Francis is a Pope who does not think primarily in spatial but in temporal categories. A social reality like the Church, the holy faithful people of God on pilgrimage through history, has to be thought of more in dynamic terms of process and relations than in static terms of substance. As he wrote in *Lumen Fidei 57*, 'Time propels toward the future and encourages us to go forward in hope.' Therefore to the project of reform based on the idea of a missionary Church which *goes forth*, corresponds the vision of an ecumenism which *goes forth* and is *on the journey*, overcoming the temptation of self-complacency and self-referential introversion. In the exchange of gifts, the Catholic Church must let itself be challenged by the other ways of being Christian and being Church, with a view to its own reform.

It is not by chance that the Exhortation points explicitly to the passage of the Decree on Ecumenism which speaks of an ongoing reform of the Church out of fidelity to Jesus Christ (*UR* 6): 'Every renewal of the Church essentially consists in an increase of fidelity to her own calling... Christ summons the Church as she goes her pilgrim way... to that continual reformation of which she always has need, insofar as she is a human institution here on earth' (*EG* 26). In the same passage Bergoglio declares his source of inspiration, none other than the Encyclical *Ecclesiam Suam* (*ES*) by Blessed Paul VI, when he said:

> The Church must look with penetrating eyes within herself, ponder the mystery of her own being... This vivid and lively self-awareness inevitably leads to a comparison between the ideal image of the Church as Christ envisaged her and loved her as his holy and spotless bride, and the actual image which the Church presents today... This is the source of the Church's heroic and impatient struggle for renewal: the struggle to correct those flaws introduced by her members which her own self-examination, mirroring her exemplar, Christ, points out to her and condemns (*ES* 3, quoted in *EG* 26).

The Church is 'the people of God on the journey.' This was the first topic in the cycle of catechesis Francis dedicated to the Church.[21] In this lesson he explained that the prehistory of the Church went back to the pages of Genesis which speak of the figure of Abraham; God chose him and asked him to set out on a journey, leave his earthly country and go to another land he would indicate. On this journey the Church too begins to set out, because when God called Abraham he was thinking of forming a people blessed by his love and through whom he would bring his blessing to all the peoples of the earth. This plan was realized in Christ and God is still realizing it today in the Church.

---

21  General audience, St Peter's Square, 18 June 2014, cf. FRANCISCO, *Pueblo de Dios en camino. Catequesis sobre la Iglesia*, Ciudad Nueva, Madrid 2014, 7-12.

In another session of his catechesis he tackled the topic of the Church's unity, commenting on the words of the Creed. Here he contrasted Jesus Christ's prayer for the unity of his disciples with our many sins against unity. Francis, who does not abandon the ideal of making progress toward full communion, dedicated his catechesis to this other problem. He described 'full communion' as 'being able to participate together in the body and blood of Christ.'[22] We can sum up this ecclesiological and ecumenical vision with some beautiful words uttered during Evening Prayer on the feast of the conversion of St Paul, which turn on this thought: 'Unity comes about on the journey; there is no wall. Unity is achieved while we are journeying.'[23]

> Christian unity – I am convinced of this – will not be the result of refined theological discussions in which each tries to convince the other of the soundness of his own opinions. The Son of Man will come and meet us even in the discussions. We need to acknowledge that to arrive at the depths. Of the mystery of God we need each other, need to meet and compare with one another under the guidance of the Holy Spirit who harmonizes diversity and overcomes conflicts, reconciles differences.

3. A third consideration can be gathered from the final sentence of this text: Francis' pastoral ecclesiology and

22 *Ibid.*, 62.
23 Cf. AAS 107 (2015) 149.

his ecumenical vision is nourished by a rich pneumatology based on this principle: the Holy Spirit overcomes division and creates unity. The Spirit gives rise to different charisms which enrich the People of God. This apparently seems to create disorder, but viewed properly, we are dealing with an enormous richness because the Holy Spirit is the Spirit of unity, and the unity does not mean uniformity. When we seek to create diversity we do so at the expense of locking ourselves into little details and then we cause divisions. When we seek unity according to our own ideas, we begin by imposing uniformity and homogeneity. Something else takes place when we allow ourselves to be guided by the Holy Spirit. He is the one who harmonizes the Church, according to the words of St Basil the Great: 'He himself is harmony' (*Ipse harmonia est*).[24]

A basic element in this pneumatological vision is the positive assessment of diversity in that it is produced by the Spirit. 'Uniformity' he said on another occasion 'is not Catholic, it is not Christian. Rather, unity in diversity. Catholic unity is different but it is one.' The Holy Spirit does two things: unity in diversity.[25] So, let us go a little further and ask ourselves how Pope St John Paul saw the logical consequences of this diversity: Why did the Holy Spirit allow all these divisions? How do we interpret the history of the one and only Church of Christ through he

---

24   Cf. Vatican website, under 'Homilies' 2014. Mass at Holy Spirit Cathedral, Istanbul, 29 November 2014. Cf. FRANCISCO, *Pueblo de Dios en camino,* 127-131; here: 129.

25   Cf. Vatican website under 'Speeches' for 2014: address to members of the Catholic Fraternity of Charismatic Covenant

tragic experience of its divisions? A first response is the uncomfortable question that comes from seeing the bitter results of sinfulness among Christians in their divisions. A second, more positive response, is the invitation to see if these divisions have also been a way that has led and still leads to the Church discovering the many riches contained in the gospel of Christ and Christ's work of redemption.[26]

Francis points to a similar explanation when he considers the existence of different tendencies of philosophical, theological and pastoral thinking as a 'variety which serves to bring about and develop different facets of the inexhaustible riches of the Gospel.' By contrast with those who dream of a monolithic teaching, he believes that these different tendencies can help to better explain the treasure of the Word and help the Church grow 'if open to being reconciled by the Spirit in respect and love' (*EG* 40). For Francis, the Holy Spirit is the one who rids us of this fear of difference which afflicts many zealous believers whose orthodoxy is based on uniformity. Multiplicity and variety, he goes on to explain, 'come from the intention of the first agent: in St Thomas's terminology. We need to grasp this variety of things in their multiple relationships. To sum up, 'we need to listen to and complement one another in our partial reception of reality and the Gospel.'[27] It is about 'recognizing what the Spirit has been sowing' in the experience and tradition of sister Churches 'as a gift for us too.'

Communities and Fellowships.

26  JOHN PAUL II, *Crossing the Threshold of Hope* Random House, New York 1995.

27  See Aquinas texts in note 44 (*EG* 40).

4. Fourthly and finally, in the light of these assumptions, we need to say a word on the Bishop of Rome who presides over the universal Church in charity. In an address on 29 June 2013, after having given the pallium to several archbishops from around the world, in the presence of a delegation from the Patriarchate of Constantinople, Francis spoke about the meaning of the Petrine ministry. He based his thoughts on the motto: '*Confirm in faith, love and unity.*'[28] Firstly, confirm in faith: the ecclesial service of Peter's successor is based on the confession of faith in Jesus Christ (Mt 16:13-18). Secondly, confirm in love: the Bishop of Rome is called to let himself be consumed by the gospel at the service of the holy and faithful people of God. Thirdly, confirm in unity: the pallium is a sign of the Church's communion, a communion which does not mean uniformity. 'We need to follow the path of synodality, to grow in harmony with the service of the primacy.' We need to continue being united in difference. This is the catholic spirit, the Christian spirit: being united in our differences.

---

28   Cf. Vatican website under 'Homilies' for 29 June 2013.

# EPILOGUE
# TIME IS GOD'S MESSENGER

The moment has come to bring a final touch to this history, in which we have intended to retrace the ecumenical journey which the Catholic Church has traversed under the guidance and impetus of Francis since the ecumenical springtime of the year of his election, to the Pentecost of the current year when he reminded us of his preeminent belief in the harmonious activity of the Paraclete: 'The same Spirit creates diversity and unity and this way shapes a new people which is varied and one: the universal Church.'[1] In accordance with our prologue we will close these pages with an epilogue of Ignatian flavour, by indicating a range of attitudes so we do not lose hope on the way toward full communion: 'Go to the land I will give you.'

## 1. *A mental representation of place*

In reality, for Jorge Mario Bergoglio, 'ecumenism can be seen as a contribution to the unity of the human family' (*EG* 245) at this time of globalization. Submitted to gospel discernment, the phenomenon of globalization is highly ambiguous (cf. *EG* 62). At no time like the present has humanity had the possibility of establishing a multicultural, polyfaceted and mutually binding world community.

---

1  FRANCIS, *Homily at Mass for Pentecost*, 4 June 2017.

Many factors lead to the suppression of cultural barriers through acceptance of the diversity of situation, race, gender or culture. However, indifference before growing social inequities, the unilateral imposition of the values and customs by some powerful culture in economic terms, the ecological crisis and the exclusion of millions of human beings from the benefits of development seriously question the process of globalization.

In his conversation with Jewish Rabbi Skorka, he took a simple but intuitive look at the problem, which brings us to the image he always prefers when thinking of peace and unity in society: 'If we conceive of globalization as a billiard ball, then the rich virtues of each culture are obliterated. The real globalization we have to defend is like the figure of a polyhedron where everything is integrated but each part retains its peculiarity which, in turn, enriches the others.'[2]

The establishment of a caring and fraternal human family continues to be a great utopian dream. Making progress in building up humanity in peace, justice and fraternity is an arduous task which Francis understands as 'the growth of a peaceful and multifaceted culture of encounter' (*EG* 220).

## 2. Put a good interpretation on another's statement rather than condemning it as false

Hence this true growth in humanity's awareness can only be achieved when based on the practice of dialogue and love. Ecumenical dialogue is a specific approach which

---

2  Cf. BERGOGLIO-SKORKA, *Sobre el cielo y la tierra*, 149 (*On Heaven and Earth* ...).

is of exceptional interest in the Pope's missionary program, because 'commitment to a unity which helps them to accept Jesus Christ can no longer be a matter of mere diplomacy or forced compliance, but rather an indispensable path to evangelization' (*EG* 246).

Evangelization begins with the experience of dialogue and encounter, person to person, a daily task which is up to all of us (*EG* 127-129). With help from a text in St Ignatius' *Spiritual Exercises* we can express in paradigmatic form our prior, open and positive disposition toward the words and attitudes of others, a sincere seeking out of others, a predisposition to dialogue, with loving recognition of the other as other, meaning acceptance of diversity. I refer to his so-called Presupposition where Ignatius says:

> It is necessary to suppose that every good Christian is more ready to put a good interpretation on another's statement than to condemn it as false. If an orthodox interpretation cannot be put on a proposition, the one who made it should be asked how he understands it. If he is in error he should be corrected in all kindness. If this does not suffice, all appropriate means should be used to bring him to a correct interpretation, and so defend the proposition from error. (*SE* no 22).

The Decree on Ecumenism has invited us to have this attitude in a dialogue of conversion and an examination of conscience (cf. *UR* 4). 'Christian unity is possible' St John

Paul II wrote, 'provided that we are humbly conscious of having sinned against unity and are convinced of our need for our conversion' (*UUS* 34; cf. 82). The Holy Spirit invites us to a serious examination of conscience. In order to establish ecumenical dialogue, repentance and conversion of heart are required. The dialogue of conversion is a prior condition for true ecumenical dialogue which demands examination of conscience, confession of our sins, repentance, being in God's grace in this 'interior space where Christ, the source of the Church's unity can effectively act with all the power of his Spirit, the Paraclete' (*UUS* 35). Francis situates himself expressly within this model. He did this in the presence of the delegation of Old Catholic bishops from the Utrecht Union, asking both sides for 'a profound spirit of inner conversion, mutual forgiveness and humble repentance.'[3]

This ecumenism of conversion which inspires the spirit of the Decree on Ecumenism and the Encyclical *Ut Unum Sint*, finds deep roots in Francis' spiritual formation. Not for nothing does the first step in the Spiritual Exercises ask one to feel and experience the mystery of sin before the crucified Lord. Faced with the question 'Who is Jorge Mario Bergoglio?' the Jesuit Pope replies: 'I am a sinner whom the Lord has looked upon.' This experience of sin and of God's superabundant grace has been captured on his episcopal coat of arms: *Miserando atque eligendo*. This motto, as has been explained on a number of occasions, was taken from the *Homilies* of St Bede the Venerable when commenting

---

3   Cf. Vatican website under 'Speeches', 30 October, 2014.

on Matthew's call: 'Jesus saw a tax collector, looked at him mercifully, and invited him to follow him.'[4]

Recently the Pope confessed that his whole spiritual life is inscribed in Chapter 16 of Ezekiel, in the final verses: 'I will establish my covenant with you, and shall know that I am the LORD, in order that you may remember and be confounded, and never open your mouth again because of your shame, when I forgive you all that you have done.'[5] Amid the perception of his own unworthiness, recognized before God's mercy, as a saved sinner whoever makes the Exercises is invited to seek and fulfil the divine will.

## 3. *The path of discernment as a means of governing*

All this is very much in harmony with the 22<sup>nd</sup> General Chapter of the Jesuits held in 1974 under Superior General Fr Pedro Arrupe, which Jorge Mario Bergoglio took part in as Provincial in Argentina. The second decree approved by that assembly begins with the question: What does it mean to be a Jesuit? The reply goes like this: 'It means recognizing that one is a sinner and, however, called to be a companion of Jesus, as was St Ignatius.' Along with this decree, focused on the question of identity, the fourth decree tackled the question of the Jesuit mission in today's world.

After a laborious process of discernment the Chapter expressed its 'fundamental option' in these terms: 'The Jesuit's

---

[4] Cf. A SPADARO Interview with Pope Francis. Cf w2.vatican.va/content/francesco/en/speeches/2013/september/documents/papa-francesco_20130921_intervista-spadaro.html

[5] Cf. U JONSSON, *Intervista a Papa Francesco*, 324.

mission today is the service of faith, for which promotion of justice is an absolute need inasmuch as it forms part of the reconciliation of means demanded by the reconciliation of the same with God.' This decision is profoundly in sync with the Apostolic Exhortation *Evangelii Nuntiandi*, so loved and praised by Pope Francis for its way of understanding evangelization.

Bergoglio confessed that one of the reasons for his becoming a Jesuit was the missionary character of the Order founded by St Ignatius. And when they asked him what is the aspect of Ignatian spirituality which has helped him most in his Petrine ministry, he replies without hesitation, discernment.[6]

The Apostolic Exhortation *Evangelii Gaudium* is a good example of this: before speaking of evangelizing activity it begins with a *gospel-based discernment*, a look at the reality in the light and strength of the Holy Spirit (*EG* 50). Discernment is an interior attitude aimed at seeking God's will, which helps us to be open to dialogue, encounter, to seeking God in daily life. It requires that these actions and discussions of ours be accompanied by a careful reading of the signs of the times (*EG* 51), of the reality which is always greater than the idea.

In his conversation with Spadaro he described this on two occasions. Firstly he said that 'for Ignatius it is an instrument of struggle in order to know the Lord and follow him more closely.' Secondly, he went back to a maximum

---

6 Cf. A SPADARO Interview with Pope Francis. A SPADARO, *La reforma de la Iglesia según Francisco. Las raíces ignacianas*, in: *La*

with which St Ignatius' view of things is usually described: *Non coerceri maximo sed contineri minimo divinum est,* which the Pope reinterpreted thus: 'It is important not to be restricted by a large space, and it is important to be able to stay in restricted spaces. That means being able to do the little things of every day with a big heart open to God and to others. That means being able to appreciate the small things inside large horizons, those of the kingdom of God.'[7] This motto, which is in fact part of the epitaph composed for an anonymous 17th Century Jesuit, was commented on by Bergoglio in a spiritual *chat* (from 1981) which he called *Conducir en lo grande y en lo peque*ño (Managing the big and the small). On that occasion he translated the maxim this way: 'Do not be intimidated by what is great, but also take account of the smallest things. That is God's way.'[8] This epitaph contains a paradoxical form of logic: that we not be afraid of the horizon of great understandings, but nor do we despise the little things. We can draw up great plans without attending to the concrete means for realizing them, or we can be caught up in the little things of each moment without being able to go beyond them to God's plan for things.

Bergoglio turns the epitaph into a criterion of basic discernment: let us be aware that while always seeking what will most lead us to God, it is not to be identified with either

*reforma y las reformas en la Iglesia*, 33-50; here: 36-45 (*Reforms of the Church. Reform in in the Church …* ).

7   Cf. A SPADARO Interview with Pope Francis.
8   Cf. JM BERGOGLIO, *Meditaciones para religiosos*, Ediciones

the biggest or the smallest. Hence the essential ambiguity of life can be redeemed for God by means of discernment. This maxim helps us adopt the most correct approach for thinking about the things pertaining to God 'from his point of view.' It is a principle not mentioned explicitly in *Evangelii Gaudium*. However we hear its echo in the passage where he explains that the whole is greater than the part: 'There is no need, then, to be overly obsessed with limited and particular questions. We constantly have to broaden our horizons and see the greater good which will benefit us all. But this has to be done without evasion or uprooting. We need to sink our roots deeper into the fertile soil and history of our native place, which is a gift of God. We can work on a small scale, in our own neighbourhood, but with a larger perspective' (*EG* 235).

According to St Ignatius' style of governing we need to know how to enflesh the great principles in the circumstances of 'place, time and people.' Francis distrusts decisions taken suddenly and is convinced that changes and reforms need this time for discernment. 'Discernment in the Lord' the Pope concludes, 'guides me in my manner of governing.'

*4. 'Going ahead in patience': time is greater than space.*

The current Pope lives in a constant dynamic of discernment, which makes him look to the future with hope. We have already indicated the profound significance of 'the journey' in his spiritual reasoning. Humanity has

Diego de Torres, Buenos Aires 1982, 114-127. See also: *En Él solo la esperanza*, 51 (*In Him Alone is Our Hope* … ).

always thought of life as a journey. The condition of *homo viator* is a constant reality in the Bible and in the history and mythology of other peoples. Setting out on a journey is rooted in an inner restlessness which brings us to 'go out of ourselves': 'Journeying in hope is being certain that the Father will give us what is needed. It is trust in the gift well beyond all calamity or misfortune.'[9] With this hopeful attitude we need to pursue the ecumenical journey.

Time and again, Francis sends us back to the biblical message of patience, of the capacity for hope, of endurance and resistance. It is a characteristic feature of the evangelizing community which accompanies humanity in lengthy, tough and prolonged processes: 'It is familiar with patient expectation and apostolic endurance,' because' evangelization consists mostly of patience and disregard for constraints of time' (*EG* 24). Time is the expression of the horizon that opens up before us and looks toward fullness. However, we have to know how to live in the moment, which is the expression of the limits we find ourselves in. Bergoglio uses a beautiful expression in his interview (which became a book) with Rubin and Ambrogetti. It is how he overcomes the tension between fullness and limits: 'going ahead in patience.' 'Going ahead in patience is realizing that time is what makes things mature. Going ahead in patience is letting time guide and kneed our lives.'[10]

---

9   Cf. FRANCISCO, *Educar: exigencia y pasión. Desafíos para educadores cristianos*, Publicaciones Claretianas, Madrid 2013, 185.
10   S RUBIN – F AMBROGETTI, *El Papa Francisco. Conversaciones con Jorge Bergoglio*, Ediciones B, Barcelona 2013.

In the search for full unity and communion between Christians, going ahead in patience means accepting that life is a continual process of learning. Up till now it has bought us and continues to bring us receptive ecumenism. The exchange of gifts is a laborious process of learning from others.

In the final chapter of the aforementioned book, Rubin and Ambrogetti put these questions to him: Is it utopian to think of the reunification of Christianity? Do you believe that the reunification of Christian Confessions will make progress? Francis' reply is as follows:

> I begin by celebrating the steps that have been taken and are being taken with the ecumenical movement. Catholics and Evangelicals feel closer, coexisting with their differences. They are seeking a reconciled diversity. Going directly to the question: I reject that for now we can think of uniformity or full unity, but of a reconciled unity which implies journeying together, praying and working together and together seeking encounter in truth.

Our Jesuit Pope likes to recall a line from St Peter Faber who says that 'Time is God's messenger' (*EG* 171). It is another way of formulating his most decisive principle: time is greater than space. It is a way of not confusing optimism with hope, which is a theological virtue, and God is involved.

English translation: *Pope Francis: Conversations with Jorge Bergoglio...*).

www.ingramcontent.com/pod-product-compliance
Lightning Source LLC
Chambersburg PA
CBHW051952290426
44110CB00015B/2208